Thank you for Hostessing
Thanksgiving –
Love you – Merraw

D1435879

90 Devotions on Nature from

OUR DAILY BREAD.

Creation
Sings
His Praise

DISCOVERY HOUSE
PUBLISHERS

© 2012 by RBC Ministries
All rights reserved.

Discovery House Publishers is affiliated with RBC Ministries,
Grand Rapids, Michigan

Requests for permission to quote from this book should be directed to:
Permissions Department, Discovery House Publishers,
P.O. Box 3566, Grand Rapids, MI 49501,
or contact us by e-mail at permissionsdept@dhp.org

All Scripture quotations, unless otherwise indicated,
are taken from the New King James Version.
©1982, Thomas Nelson, Inc., Publishers.
Use by permission. All rights reserved.

Cover and interior design by Mark Veldheer

ISBN: 978-1-57293-567-9

Printed in the United States of America

First printing in 2012

CONTENTS

Foreword by Mart DeHaan 5

The Closer We Look 6
The Challenge of the Woodpecker 7
Fast Food and the Phalarope 8
Clem the Cat 10
Puddle Ducks and Divers 11
Learning from Bullet 12
Pride's Penalty 13
Helpful Honks 15
The Restless Sea 16
Musings on a Wintry Day 17
You Are Unique! 18
L. L. Bean's Golden Rule 19
Don't Lose Your Head 20
The Tomcat and the Tree 22
What the Canoe Can't Do 23
Singing at Night 24
Echoes of Paradise 25
The Right Tool 28
Sandal Love 29
The Ant Lions 30
The Legend of the Pelican 31
Keep Walking 33
Hope for the Helpless 34
Deceit and a Smart Dog 35
Making Tracks 36
First Pride—Then the Fall 37
Learning from the Redwoods 38
Of Birds and Stars 40
The Spring That Satisfies 41
When the Star Falls 42
Who—or What—Do We Thank? 43
Open Wide 45
The Hidden Rattler 46
Bound to Be Free 47
"Bee" Happy? 48
What's with the Loons? 49
Flying Backward 52
He Can Be Trusted 53
Ants, Antifreeze, and Adoration 54
The Right View of Jesus 55
The God of the Beautiful 56
Stay in the Light 58
Tough Trees 59
New Songs 60
Stop the Slide 61
A Life-and-Death Matter 63

The High Cost of Getting Even 64
Shark Tonic 65
"Try Some Ducks" 66
The Wonder of Nature 67
Lion of Judah 68
Redwood Support 70
Seeing God 71
The Devil's Soup Bowl 72
"Seasons" Greetings 73
Michael Cardinal 76
Johnny Appleseed 77
The Warbler's Witness 78
Where's the Power? 79
Call of the Chickadee 81
No God? 82
A Walk with Whitaker 83
Weed Control 84
Lost in the Fog 85
By Dawn's Early Light 86
A Common Enemy 88
Light of Creation 89
A Sad Split 90
Register Rock 91
Giants of the Deep 93
Show Your Colors 94
The Rock and the Flourishing Palms . . . 95
Springboard of Praise 96
A Path Through the Woods 97
Elephants Down 100
Man-Made Hail 101
God and the Ravens 102
Embroidery of Earth 103
God's Signature 104
Of Flies and Sparrows 106
Bombardier Beetle 107
"Dead Sea" Christian? 108
Little Sponges 109
Be Careful! 111
Creation: NT Style 112
Of Ants and Elephant Seals 113
You Can Count on It! 114
Einstein's God 115
The Opened Hand 118
Good to Be Home 119

Scripture Index 120
Our Daily Bread Writers 122
Note to the Reader 128

FOREWORD

Several years ago an international team of astronomers announced that images from the Hubble Space Telescope had given evidence of 40,000 galaxies in a window of the night sky no larger than the size of the moon.

Since then, in a basement laboratory of Canada's Victoria University, another group of scientists has been working to build the most powerful microscope in human history. When operational, it should give researchers a closer look at a subatomic universe by exploring an inner space that appears to be as boundlessly small as outer space is inexpressibly great.

Meanwhile, the ancient prophet Isaiah continues to say from the pages of the Bible, "'To whom then will you liken Me, or to whom shall I be equal?' says the Holy One. Lift up your eyes on high, and see who has created these things" (Isaiah 40:25–26).

By the silent witness of the natural world and the inspired words of the messenger, we are awakened to a God for whom no problem is too great and no detail is too small. So the prophet goes on to say:

> The everlasting God, the Lord,
> 　　The Creator of the ends of the earth,
> Neither faints nor is weary.
> 　　His understanding is unsearchable.
> He gives power to the weak,
> 　　And to those who have no might He increases strength…
> But those who wait on the Lord
> 　　Shall renew their strength;
> They shall mount up with wings like eagles,
> 　　They shall run and not be weary,
> 　　They shall walk and not faint (40:28–29, 31).

May the thoughts within this special Nature edition of *Our Daily Bread* deepen our gratefulness for what our God has done for us. May we be renewed in the wonders of His creation, in the wisdom of His inspired words, and, above all, in the love of the Creator who died for us.

—Mart DeHaan, *RBC Ministries*

The Closer We Look…

Guidebook Reading: Ecclesiastes 7:20–29

Consider the work of God; for who can make straight what He has made crooked?
—ECCLESIASTES 7:13

After God completed His six days of activity in creation, He took a look at what He had accomplished. Genesis 1:31 says, "God saw everything that He had made, and indeed it was very good." Later, Moses said of God: "He is the Rock, His work is perfect" (Deuteronomy 32:4). These words of excellence apply to everything God has made—and they are true of His Word as well.

Fact of Nature

Lilies are beautiful, but they can be poisonous to cats. The flower contains a toxin that can cause kidney failure in felines.

God's work can stand the most intense inspection. The more carefully we view God's work (including His Word), the more its perfection becomes evident. This is especially true if we inspect it microscopically. When we investigate what God has made, we always find new and greater things about which to wonder and marvel.

For instance, if we dissect a flower and observe it closely, new beauties of design and purpose unfold before us. The more we study it, the more delicate patterns and veins we see—intricacies of beauty and function that completely escape the naked eye.

I had the opportunity to examine a simple blossom by placing it under a magnifying glass. Through that, I came to appreciate as never before the words of our Lord, "Consider the lilies . . . even Solomon in all his glory was not arrayed like one of these" (Luke 12:27).

This perfection of content and design also applies to the Word of God in a special way. Nature is clouded by sin, but the Scriptures—by the power of inspiration—are inerrant. The more we study the Word of the Lord, the more its wisdom and beauty is evident. We should never grow tired of examining God's perfect book.

—*M. R. DeHaan*

✳ COMPASS POINT

Examine God's work and His Word—and you'll find perfection.

The Challenge of the Woodpecker

Guidebook Reading: Psalm 104:10–24

"Many, O LORD my God, are Your wonderful works which You have done."
—PSALM 40:5

The woodpecker is an amazing bird! It has been equipped with sharp, curved claws and a powerful drill-like beak. Its stiff, spiny tail feathers are designed for propping and bracing the colorful creature as it delivers hundreds of rapid and forceful beak-strokes into the bark of trees in search of beetles and insect eggs. Once a hole is made in the wood, the bird's long, slender, sticky tongue is deftly inserted to remove the desired grubs.

How a woodpecker can slam its head so violently against a solid object without destroying itself is still a mystery. Scientists say its skull is reinforced inside with a mini shock-absorber system, a small brain, and softer bones, all of which account in part for its ability to withstand such unusual "punishment." Author Fred J. Meldau wrote:

Fact of Nature

Woodpeckers' nostrils are covered with bristlelike feathers that prevent them from inhaling particles of wood as they drill holes. God thinks of everything.

Surely every woodpecker in the world is a living witness to the fact that God made it as it is. Evolution can in no wise explain how it got its unique tongue [unlike any other bird's tongue, it curls around the skull], its specially constructed tail, its unusual feet, and above all its marvelous chisel-like beak! That such amazing equipment was perfected through long ages of "gradual change" is a preposterous assumption. Any specialized organ—like the tongue, or beak, or tail, of the woodpecker—must be perfectly "adapted" before it serves its intended purpose. A beak that is only half developed . . . or a tongue only one-tenth as long as it needs to be to reach a grub hidden inside the trunk of a tree, would be absolutely useless. If specialized organs came to pass through the process of gradual change, due to "random mutations," what purpose did they serve while they were in the process of "developing"?

The woodpecker. A noisy but effective illustration of God's "wonderful works."

—*Henry Bosch*

✦ COMPASS POINT

The evidence of God's creation is spellbinding.

Fast Food and the Phalarope

Guidebook Reading: Psalm 104:23–35

What You give them they gather in; You open Your hand, they are filled with good.
—PSALM 104:28

An item in *National Geographic* magazine carried this caption: "New Spin on Fast Food." The article was about the phalarope, "a wading shorebird that has a unique way of dining on creatures too deep for it to reach." Spinning in the water at breakneck speed—a full spin per second—it creates a vortex that "pumps up" shrimp from a depth of three feet.

Fact *of* Nature

There are three kinds of phalaropes: red phalarope, red-necked phalarope, and Wilson's phalarope.

According to UCLA biologist William M. Hamner, the bird is also a speedy eater. His research team has learned that "phalaropes detect prey, thrust, seize, transport, and swallow in less than half a second, at a rate of 180 pecks per minute."

The author of Psalm 104 probably never saw a phalarope, but he had observed enough of God's creative genius in nature to fill his heart with praise. He wrote:

> *The earth is full of Your possessions . . .*
> *Living things both small and great . . .*
> *These all wait for You,*
> *That You may give them their food in due season.*
> *What You give them they gather in (vv. 24–28).*

Do we think of our life-support systems—the food we eat, the air we breathe, the strength we receive—as coming from the hand of God? Most of us take these provisions for granted. With your Bible open to Psalm 104, look again at the marvels of God's world.

—*Dennis DeHaan*

✳ COMPASS POINT

Contemplate the richness of God's earthly provisions.

Clem the Cat

Guidebook Reading: Jeremiah 8:4–7

Why has this people slidden back, Jerusalem, in perpetual backsliding? . . .
They refuse to return. —JEREMIAH 8:5

Clem the cat came home after eight years of being who-knows-where. A homeowner in Bancroft, Wisconsin, said he heard a cat meowing on the front porch. When he opened the door, a big, long-haired gray male cat walked in, checked things out, began purring, and then jumped up on his favorite chair. Family members couldn't believe their eyes. But when they compared the cat to pictures taken eight years earlier, they could only conclude that Clem had come home.

What remarkable homing instincts God has given to some animals! On a spiritual level, why is it that the backslidden child of God seems to have less? Why do we in our rebellion show less sense than the animals? We've been designed by a loving Creator who has given us every reason to want to come home. In His presence there is love, lasting protection, and fullness of joy. Away from Him there is temporary pleasure, but lasting loss. Inside there is hope. Outside there is despair.

Jeremiah reminded us that even the birds live according to the times and places and ways that the Lord has built into them (Jeremiah 8:7). Only man seems determined to run to his own self-destruction.

Father, forgive us for running away from you. Lead us back to yourself today.

—*Mart DeHaan*

Fact *of* Nature

Vivian Oxley of Plymouth, England, took her dog Jarvis across Plymouth Sound to a park near Cremyll, but he ran off. After searching for him unsuccessfully, she sadly took the ferry back to Plymouth. Shortly thereafter, Jarvis showed up at home. He had apparently taken the ferry on his own and made his way back for a happy reunion.

✳ COMPASS POINT

No matter what we have done, we can always be forgiven and return to God's loving arms.

Puddle Ducks and Divers

Guidebook Reading: Psalm 1

His delight is in the law of the LORD, and in His law he meditates day and night.
—PSALM 1:2

To know God better, we must grow in our knowledge of the Bible. Through its pages we learn not only facts about Him but also how to know Him personally. It is only reasonable, then, that we should spend time reading God's Word to gain information about God and meditating on it so we can plumb its depths.

When I began to paint duck decoys, I learned that there are two kinds of ducks: puddle ducks and divers. Puddle ducks, such as mallards and redheads, simply paddle around the edge of marshes and ponds and feed in the shallow water. They eat only what they can reach from the surface. Diver ducks, however, are able to dive to surprising depths in a lake to feed from the plants at its bottom. Mergansers and canvasbacks are typical of this group, some of which can dive to depths of 150 feet for their food!

> ## Fact *of* Nature
>
> One thing that distinguishes the merganser duck from others is that it has a serrated bill.

There are also two kinds of Christians—at least when it comes to studying the Scriptures. Some, like puddle ducks, stay near the surface, satisfied with the nourishment they find in the shallows. Others, however, are like divers. Following the example of the psalmist, they plunge deeply into the Word through study, reflection, and meditation "day and night."

Which are you—a puddle duck or a diver? Have you established a satisfying, deepening study of God's Word? Or are you content to stay near the surface? What about it? Is it time to begin going a little deeper?

—*Dave Egner*

✳ COMPASS POINT
Dive into God's Word and meditate on it.

Learning from Bullet

Guidebook Reading: 1 Timothy 4:1–5

Now the Spirit expressly says that in latter times some will depart from the faith, giving heed to deceiving spirits and doctrines of demons, speaking lies in hypocrisy, having their own conscience seared with a hot iron. —1 TIMOTHY 4:1–2

Dogs are usually rather intelligent animals, but Charles Medley of Rockford, Illinois, had some doubts about his dog Bullet. Whenever Bullet heard a squirrel, a rabbit, or a person, he would take off like a shot in the direction of that sound. It didn't matter that he was tied up. By the time he reached the end of his rope, he'd be traveling at maximum velocity, heading straight for his target. But in an instant, his strong rope would pull taut and jerk Bullet to a jarring, sprawling halt. That beagle never learned his limits.

God has built into us a moral tug on the soul whenever we go beyond what is good for us. It's called conscience. Unlike Bullet's rope, however, it doesn't stop us from going too far. Furthermore, conscience can be deadened when we violate it repeatedly, and it can be programmed with wrong information so that we may feel guilty when no real guilt exists—or we may be guilty and not feel it.

We must learn the moral limits God places on us for our own good and then choose to live within those limits. If we read God's Word and trust the Holy Spirit to teach us, our conscience becomes attuned to His standard of right and wrong. This helps us to know our limits. If we live within them, we can experience great freedom and joy each day.

—*Dennis DeHaan*

Fact *of* Nature

Beagles are great tracking dogs; in fact, if they get onto a scent, nothing short of a fence or a leash will stop them from tracking it far from home.

 COMPASS POINT

The Bible is our all-important life-guide.

Pride's Penalty

Guidebook Reading: Proverbs 29:14–23

A man's pride will bring him low. — PROVERBS 29:23

An old fable tells of two ducks and a frog that often played together in a small pond on a farm. When the hot summer days arrived, the pond shrank to a small puddle, and they were forced to move. The ducks could easily fly to another place, but not their friend. Finally, the frog suggested that the ducks put a stick in their bills so that he could cling to it with his mouth as they flew away.

The little amphibian was very proud of his shrewd idea. As the three of them took off for a nearby lake, they passed over a farmer, who looked up and said, "Well, isn't that a clever stunt! I wonder who thought of it?" Swelling with pride, the frog shouted, "I did!" And in that instant he lost his grip on the stick and went crashing to the ground.

> ## Fact *of* Nature
>
> The good news is that, according to most reports, ducks do not eat frogs.

Many people have met defeat in spite of their great learning and knowledge because of a haughty, arrogant spirit. A good example is King Nebuchadnezzar, mentioned in the book of Daniel. He headed up a mighty kingdom that is associated with Babylon's Hanging Gardens, one of the seven wonders of the ancient world. But instead of giving the Lord the glory, he exclaimed, "Is not this great Babylon, that I have built . . . by my mighty power and for the honor of my majesty?" (Daniel 4:30). As a result, God punished him by letting him lose his reason. He became like a beast and ate grass like an ox. His "body was wet with the dew of heaven till his hairs had grown like eagles' feathers and his nails like birds' claws" (v. 33).

Beware of pride. It will lead to a painful deflation of the ego and a humbling defeat. Praise goes to God—not ourselves.

—*Henry Bosch*

✷ COMPASS POINT

Humility looks better on you than pride does.

Helpful Honks

Guidebook Reading: Romans 15:1–6

We then who are strong ought to bear with the scruples of the weak, and not to please ourselves. —ROMANS 15:1

Each fall we are visited by flocks of migrating geese that stop off at a meadow near our home. For several weeks those birds fly in long, wavy V-formations over our house, honking as they go. But then, as winter approaches, they are off again on their long flight south.

A student of mine furthered my education of, and my appreciation for, these visitors from the north. He told me that the geese fly at speeds of forty to fifty miles per hour. They travel in formation because as each bird flaps its wings, it creates an updraft for the bird behind it. Geese can go 70 percent farther in a group than they could if they were to fly alone.

Christians are like that in a way. When we have a common purpose, we are propelled by the thrust of others who share those same goals. We can get a lot farther together than we can alone.

As geese fly, they also honk at one another— not as critics but as encouragers. Some say that those in the rear sound off to exhort those up front to stay on course and maintain their speed. We too move ahead much more easily if there is someone behind us encouraging us to stay on track and keep going.

Is there someone flying in formation with you today to whom you might give some "helpful honks"?

—*Haddon Robinson*

Fact *of* Nature

If a goose in a formation is injured, one or two other geese will stay behind with the downed bird until it either dies or is ready to fly again.

✳ COMPASS POINT

There is great value in encouraging other people.

The Restless Sea

Guidebook Reading: Isaiah 57:15–21

The wicked are like the troubled sea, when it cannot rest, whose waters cast up mire and dirt. — ISAIAH 57:20

I fight a losing battle with black silt on the lake bottom near our cabin in Michigan's Upper Peninsula. In the morning before my grandchildren awaken, I rake the lake bottom close to the dock so they can wade on clean sand.

It works well—until noon. That's when the power boaters begin to run, pulling an assortment of people on a variety of tubes and skis. They make waves, which carry fresh silt to the shore. Even when no high-speed craft appear, the wind usually rises about then, creating neat little whitecaps. They too stir up the silt and deposit it, covering the cleared lake bottom with black gunk and littering it with debris.

Imagine a sea that is always churning with turbulence. The foaming restlessness never quiets, sending up plumes of dirt and mire. Isaiah described the wicked that way (57:20). Their lives are like a frothy, wave-tossed, unsettled, restless sea—never calm, never at peace (v. 21).

Peace is available to all who believe in Christ. Not only can we be at peace with God but we can also have the peace of God firmly settled in our hearts (John 14:27).

If you don't have peace, if you are worn out by the turbulence of unrest, turn in faith to Jesus. He has the power to calm the restless sea of your life.

—*Dave Egner*

Fact of Nature

Speaking of churning water—one of the most dangerous waves in the world is the Banzai Pipeline off Oahu Island in Hawaii. Its 12-foot waves have claimed the lives of both surfers and photographers who try to brave its fury.

✳ COMPASS POINT

Peace. Who doesn't want it? God offers it.

Musings on a Wintry Day

Guidebook Reading: Psalm 147

He gives to the beast its food, and to the young ravens that cry. — PSALM 147:9

One bitterly cold morning I looked out the back window and saw as many as twenty feathered friends congregating around our birdfeeder. Some were busily eating seeds while others were pecking away at a piece of suet fastened to a tree. Later, when I stepped out the front door, I saw our German shepherd romping in the snow with two canine friends who visited her almost every day. I don't know if dogs can smile, but all three surely looked happy. On my way to the office, I drove past a field where four American bison were lying on the ground, a picture of contentment and comfort. They were obviously well-fed, and like the birds and the dogs, they seemed oblivious to the cold.

As I reflected upon all of this, Psalm 147 came to my mind. The inspired writer of this beautiful Hebrew song extols the goodness and greatness of God. After declaring God's mercy to Israel, he pictures the Almighty directing those mysterious processes by which rain is provided for the earth. He portrays the grass springing up on the hillsides and says that beasts of burden, domesticated cattle, and even wild creatures like ravens receive their food from the hand of their Creator. The writer gives us a picture of winter and spring, billowy white piles of snow, the gray-white film of hoarfrost, ice-covered streams, warming breezes, and free-flowing waters. All of this takes place at the command of God. He speaks, and all nature obeys. The psalmist closes with the words, "Praise the Lord!"

I thought, *How wonderful He is!* And as I parked my car, I said, "Hallelujah!"

—*Herb Vander Lugt*

Fact *of* Nature

In the winter the American bison develops an extra thick layer of fur to protect itself against the cold because it does not migrate to a warmer climate. The current bison population in the US is approximately 350,000.

COMPASS POINT

Praise God! He controls the natural world.

You Are Unique!

Guidebook Reading: Romans 12:3–8

For as we have many members in one body . . . having then gifts differing according to the grace that is given to us, let us use them. —ROMANS 12:4–6

The bison, the great beast of the American plains, was designed in such a way that its natural inclination is to look down. The anatomy of a bison's neck makes it difficult for it to look up. In contrast, giraffes, which grace the savannas of Africa, are designed in a way that makes looking up easy. The way a giraffe's neck was made makes it difficult for it to look down. Two creatures created by the same God but with distinctively different body parts and purposes. Giraffes eat leaves from branches above. Bison eat grass from the field below. God provides food for both, and neither has to become like the other to eat.

As we observe the animals and people around us, we're reminded that God made each of us unique for a purpose. One person's natural tendency is to look up and see the "big picture," while another looks down and focuses on details. Both are important. One is not better than the other. God gave us each individual talents and spiritual gifts so we can work together as a body.

Human beings are the crowning jewel of creation, and we shine the brightest not when we see our own likeness reflected in others but when each of us performs the unique functions that God designed for us to do. "Having then gifts differing according to the grace that is given to us, let us use them" (Romans 12:6).

—*Julie Ackerman Link*

Fact of Nature

Aided by their long legs, giraffes can run up to 35 miles an hour for short distances. That's about half as fast as a cheetah can run. A bison is a bit slower at 30 mph.

✳ COMPASS POINT

Every person is unique—and qualified for a specific task.

L. L. Bean's Golden Rule

Guidebook Reading: Luke 6:27–36

Whatever you want men to do to you, do also to them. — MATTHEW 7:12

More than a hundred years ago, Leon Leonwood Bean started a business in Freeport, Maine, based on this simple premise: "Sell good merchandise at a reasonable profit, treat your customers like human beings, and they'll always come back for more." Thus L. L. Bean got its start selling a variety of outdoor apparel, sporting goods, and camping equipment. From the beginning, every item was unconditionally guaranteed. If a customer was dissatisfied, he could return any item at any time for any reason.

I don't know if Mr. Bean was a Christian, but his "golden rule" is very close to what Jesus taught in the Sermon on the Mount. Bean thought it was his duty to provide quality merchandise and to treat his customers like human beings. All this sounds like "whatever you want men to do to you, do also to them."

Jesus always put people above things and manmade laws. He enhanced human dignity by seeking the physical and spiritual well-being of everyone He met. We who know Him as Savior have the Holy Spirit to help us follow His example, whether in business, at school, or at home. If this produces "profit" and wins the favor of others, we should humbly accept it as God's blessing. But if not—and sometimes it won't—we must practice it anyway. Why? Because that's the way Christ treats us, and He wants to treat others that way through us.

The Golden Rule is still the best answer to the selfishness and greed that plagues this sinful, old world we live in.

—*Dennis DeHaan*

Fact *of* Nature

Leon Bean's first product was a "waterproof" boot for fishermen. It wasn't so waterproof, and 90 percent of his initial boots were returned (the people got their money back, of course).

✳ COMPASS POINT

Treat others the right way.

Don't Lose Your Head

Guidebook Reading: Proverbs 6:20–35

My son, keep my words, and treasure my commands . . . that they may keep you from the immoral woman. —PROVERBS 7:1, 5

The praying mantis is one of the more outstanding insects of the garden, if for no other reason than its large size. But the most fascinating characteristic about this unique creature is that a mantis "in love" is a lot like a man caught in the grip of lust. The instinct that sends the male mantis in pursuit of a mate often results in its untimely death.

I watched this happen some time ago on an interesting TV nature program that portrayed the unusual habits of this remarkable insect. In one instance, an attracted male tried to show affection for a lady mantis, but she viciously attacked him. And in another case, a female actually accepted the attention of her "lover" but then suddenly turned cannibal. In the most literal way, the mantis that pursued her lost his head.

Fact *of* Nature

There are more than 2,000 species of praying mantises worldwide.

The Bible tells us that much the same thing can happen to us if we let our natural drives steer us in the wrong direction. If the author of Proverbs had been writing to his daughter, he probably would have warned her about the many "lines" a man uses to gain a woman's affection. He would have cautioned her never to act against her better judgment. But in this passage of Scripture, the author was writing to his son. Five times in the first nine chapters of Proverbs he told him in unmistakable terms that a man can lose his head, his heart, and his body to the power of seduction. The wrong woman is an overwhelming magnet to wrong desire.

We need to listen to those pointed admonitions, remembering that even a strong man carried away by lust can lose his head and ruin his life.

—*Mart DeHaan*

 COMPASS POINT

Lust can be deadly, so avoid it.

The Tomcat and the Tree

Guidebook Reading: Daniel 6:1–10

Now when Daniel knew that the writing was signed, he went home. And in his upper room, with his windows open toward Jerusalem, he knelt down on his knees three times that day. —DANIEL 6:10

The humorous story is told of a farmer who had a tomcat that was especially terrified by barking dogs. Often a friendly neighbor would come to visit, bringing along his two hounds. Whenever the cat heard the trio approaching, he would dash around the house and scramble up into a large evergreen that stood in the front yard.

One day the farmer cut down the tree. That evening, seeing the approach of the neighbor and his dogs, the tomcat made his usual dash around the house. It is reported he was thirty feet up before he noticed that the tree was no longer there!

Fact of Nature

Climbing trees is natural for cats, but going back down is a problem. Their claws are curved the wrong way, so until they learn to back down the tree, they get stuck.

This amusing but fictitious story illustrates an important point: an oft-repeated act becomes a habit that exerts a powerful influence! We should therefore be careful to cultivate only tendencies that are constructive and helpful.

Daniel 6 informs us that for many years Daniel prayed three times a day with the windows of his chamber opened toward Jerusalem. When the king's order outlawed this, he did not stop—even though he knew it might mean death if he continued. His action was more than mere habit, however. It was a courageous expression of faith. Kneeling to pray had become so much a part of his life that he maintained it in spite of the danger.

Regular prayer at stated times, faithful attendance at church services, and daily Bible reading are habits worthy of cultivation. If you have not developed these practices as part of your pattern of life, you will need to discipline yourself for a time. Faithfully carried out, however, they will become good spiritual habits that will help you all through life.

—*Herb Vander Lugt*

✸ COMPASS POINT

Develop good spiritual discipline.

What the Canoe Can't Do

Guidebook Reading: Titus 3:1–8

Not by works of righteousness which we have done, but according to His mercy He saved us. —TITUS 3:5

If some people were to be absolutely honest, they would have to admit that they are trying to earn their way to heaven. They are putting their faith in their good intentions and admirable deeds—not in the death, burial, and resurrection of the Lord Jesus Christ. For instance, when my neighbor died, his wife said to me, "Surely he is in heaven, don't you think? He was a good man. He was such a good man." I agreed that he had been a fine husband and a conscientious father, but I had to add, "He'll be in heaven if he believed in Jesus Christ as his Savior."

I was thinking about our inability to save ourselves one afternoon when I was fishing from our fourteen-foot canoe. I decided that a person would be a fool to think he could cross the ocean through gale-force winds and swelling waves in a vessel like the one I was in. The unstable craft simply could not make it.

And our good works and worthy intentions cannot take us to heaven. Oh, our goodness may make the circumstances of this life more pleasant—just as sitting in a canoe on a calm lake is pleasant—but our goodness will never meet the just demands of a righteous God. The only solution is to put our trust in Christ. When we accept Him through faith, He gives us His righteousness—and that holiness will take us to heaven.

—*Dave Egner*

Fact of Nature

Verlen Kruger has the longest canoe trip on record: He traveled more than 28,000 miles through and around North America on the Ultimate Canoe Challenge between 1980 and 1983.

✳ COMPASS POINT

Jesus' sacrifice, not our works, gets us to heaven.

Singing at Night

Guidebook Reading: Psalm 20

No one says, "Where is God my Maker, who gives songs in the night." —Job 35:10

There are two little birds that are beautiful pictures of the spirit of song. One is the skylark. It awakens early in the morning and greets the rising monarch of the day with music. Its whole being seems to burst forth in song.

The other bird is the nightingale. This dark-colored little bird hides away in the bushes and doesn't sing much in the daytime. But when evening comes, it trills forth with its beautiful, tender, moving night song.

In the spiritual realm, as in the world of nature, the singers of the day are more numerous than the singers of the night. But surely we can glorify God the most by singing in spite of the dark.

It is not hard to praise the Lord when everything is going well, when we have our health, when the family is happy, and when we have a good job. But what happens when trials come? When our health is gone, our money is spent, relationships are broken, or tragedy strikes, the reality of our faith is tested. Only those who are wholeheartedly committed to Christ can have a song in the night.

Some of the sweetest Christians I have ever met were God's patient sufferers on their beds or in their wheelchairs who had learned to sing in the dark.

—M. R. DeHaan

Fact *of* Nature

English poets Percy Bysshe Shelley and John Keats wrote poems with these birds as their inspiration. Keats wrote his "Ode to a Nightingale" in England in 1819. Shelley's "To a Skylark" was written while he was visiting Italy in 1820 with his wife, Mary, the author of the novel *Frankenstein*.

✳ COMPASS POINT

God deserves our praise in good times and bad.

Echoes of Paradise

Guidebook Reading: Revelation 21:1–7

Behold, I make all things new. — REVELATION 21:5

"Come to paradise," says an ad featuring white sands, turquoise water, and waving palm trees. It's as if we are being given a glimpse of Eden rediscovered.

Not long ago, my wife and I took a trip to the Bahamas. Those marvelous coral-reef islands have a unique beauty. Yet for us the environment alone did not seem like paradise. Something was missing.

Then on Sunday we found what we had been looking for. We attended a church off the beaten path. The service was three hours long, but it was filled with vibrant worship. With beautiful Bahamian accents the pastor and his congregation took turns quoting Scripture throughout the sermon. My wife and I left the service energized in our faith.

I was reminded of Revelation's witness to the future chorus: "They sang as it were a new song before the throne" (14:3). One day, "God will wipe away every tear from [our] eyes; there shall be no more death, nor sorrow, nor crying" (21:4). What a day of rejoicing that will be!

Our worship here is a mere prelude to the great praise service in the future when we stand in God's presence. But sometimes when we join with others in vibrant worship, we experience an echo of paradise on this earth.

—*Dennis Fisher*

Fact of Nature

A study of the Bahamian coral reefs revealed that having a ban on fishing in the area of the reefs led to healthier coral and a more well-balanced ecosystem.

✴ COMPASS POINT

Earthly worship prepares us for ultimate worship.

The Right Tool

Guidebook Reading: Jeremiah 23:25–40

Is not My word . . . like a hammer that breaks the rock in pieces?
—JEREMIAH 23:29

I came across a fallen beech tree that would provide great firewood for the cast-iron stove in our cabin. My chainsaw cut it neatly into logs about eighteen inches long. But these twenty-inch diameter pieces still needed to be split. So I began to swing my ax. Nothing happened—except that the blade got stuck in the wood. My ax was sharp, but it wasn't heavy enough to split that kind of wood.

After an hour of frustration, I drove to the hardware store and purchased a larger, heavier tool called a splitting maul. It has an ax blade on one side of the head and a sledgehammer on the other. With the right tool, I soon had a nice stack of split firewood drying for the next year.

Sometimes I try to get God's work done by using the wrong tool. I'm great at giving my opinion in helping someone solve a problem, but often not much happens until I search out and apply God's truth to the situation.

Jeremiah condemned the false prophets in Israel because they were using the wrong tools—their own words, dreams, and visions—to influence and lead the people, rather than God's direct revelation (Jeremiah 23:16, 25–27, 31–32).

Let's do the Lord's work with the right tool—the power and authority of the Word of the living God.

—*Dave Egner*

Fact *of* Nature

Want to burn some calories? Splitting firewood can eat up between 400 and 700 calories per hour.

✸ COMPASS POINT

God gives us the equipment. It's up to us to use it.

Sandal Love

Guidebook Reading: 1 John 3:16–24

Let us not love in word or in tongue, but in deed and in truth. —1 JOHN 3:18

A young woman backpacking in Colorado encountered another woman hobbling down a mountain trail. On one foot she wore an improvised shoe made of green twigs wrapped with a strip of cloth.

"Lost one boot crossing a stream," she explained. "Hope I can get down the mountain before dark."

The first hiker reached into her own pack and took out a sport sandal. "Wear this," she said. "You can mail it to me when you get home."

The woman gratefully accepted the sandal and set off down the trail. A few days later the sandal arrived in the mail with a note: "I passed several people who noticed my predicament, but you're the only one who offered any help. It made all the difference. Thanks for sharing your sandal with me."

The Bible says love can be seen and touched— it's tangible. It may be as big as the Good Samaritan's care for an injured man (Luke 10:30–37) or as small as a cup of cold water given in Jesus' name (Matthew 10:42).

Real love takes action. The Bible says, "Let us not love in word or in tongue, but in deed and in truth" (1 John 3:18).

On the trail of life today, when we meet a hobbler, let's offer a sandal in love.

—*David McCasland*

Fact of Nature

In a recent year, Trails.com website calculated that Breakneck Ridge Trail in Hudson Highlands State Park (New York) was the most popular hiking trail in the United States.

✴ COMPASS POINT

Genuine love looks a lot like doing something for others.

The Ant Lions

Guidebook Reading: Psalm 104:24–35

These all wait for You, that You may give them their food in due season.
—Psalm 104:27

The ant lion is a little insect whose larva (also called a doodlebug) lives in regions of dry or sandy soil. It digs a pit about two inches deep and waits for ants to fall in.

The ant lion is equipped with a highly sensitive alarm system that picks up the slightest vibration. A single ant falling into its hole can activate it. Anchor-like appendages under its body enable it to grip the soil as it struggles with its victim.

Fact of Nature

An adult ant lion is an insect that looks like a small dragonfly. It is mostly dormant during the day and does its flying in the evening.

Even more remarkable is its complex mouth that forms a kind of "drinking straw," ideal for sucking fluids. When an ant is trapped, the ant lion injects it with a paralyzing drug and then with digestive juices that allows it to feed on its prey.

The eminent French zoologist Pierre-Paul Grassé says that Darwin's theory of natural selection can't explain the "avalanche of . . . chance occurrences" necessary for such a creature to evolve. Grassé's research keeps pointing toward a Creator, even though he himself remains an unbeliever.

The psalmist told us that God made all living things and feeds them, and we accept that by faith. Scientists marvel at nature's unique design, and they would not be at odds with the psalmist if they would merely believe what their findings point to—God, the great Designer.

—*Dennis DeHaan*

✴ COMPASS POINT

Nature's designs point to God.

The Legend of the Pelican

Guidebook Reading: Acts 20:17–27

None of these things move me; nor do I count my life dear to myself, so that I may finish my race with joy. —Acts 20:24

I was surprised to learn that in religious art the pelican has long been a symbol of self-sacrifice. Having observed these strange birds firsthand while fishing along the west coast of Florida, I felt that they were more like lazy freeloaders than self-denying saints. With pitiful stares that masked hearts full of envy, they would sit and lust after every fish I caught. Once in a while they would even try to intercept one before I could reel it in.

Their behavior, however, is not why they symbolize self-sacrifice. The association is made because of their red-tipped beak. According to legend, when a mother pelican cannot find food for her young, she thrusts her beak into her breast and nourishes her little ones with her own blood. The early church saw in this story a beautiful picture of what Christ did for us and what we in turn should do for one another. The apostle Paul reflected this self-giving attitude as he made his farewell speech to the Ephesian believers (Acts 20:24).

> ## Fact *of* Nature
>
> As pelicans fly over the shoreline or beach, they make a majestic sight as they extend their wingspan to 9 feet in width.

Because of our sinful nature, we are characterized more by greed than by self-sacrifice. But that can change. Through faith in Jesus we are forgiven and our hearts are transformed. Then, as we depend on God's Spirit who lives within us, we will practice the art of self-sacrificing love.

—*Mart DeHaan*

✸ COMPASS POINT

A life of self-sacrifice is admirable and desirable.

Keep Walking

Guidebook Reading: Hebrews 10:32–39

Let us lay aside every weight, and the sin which so easily ensnares us, and let us run with endurance the race that is set before us. — HEBREWS 12:1

On a warm summer afternoon, three young people and I decided to walk a five-mile stretch along the north bank of the Tahquamenon River in Michigan's Upper Peninsula. We started out with energy and vigor, taking the first few hundred yards with ease. But then the path began to twist and turn as it followed the river's course. We had to trudge through low, muddy areas and scramble up steep ridges. Fallen trees had to be climbed over or crawled under. The only way to cross some of the creeks that flowed into the river was to walk gingerly over a fallen log or to jump across. Facing one obstacle after another, we all began to slow down. We weren't sure how far we had to go or what lay ahead. Yet we knew we had friends waiting for us at the end of the trail, and we had to keep pressing on.

When we did stop for a brief rest, we talked about some parallels between our walk and the Christian's journey through life. It too has highs and lows. Difficulties of all sorts must be overcome and dangers avoided. We aren't sure what's ahead, and we get weary and discouraged. The temptation is to collapse where we are and stop going forward. But the goal is always before us, and the Bible tells us to "run with endurance."

Have you come to a standstill in your Christian life because you are discouraged and tired? Have you stopped making progress? If so, I urge you, "Don't stop now!" In God's strength, take that next step. Allow Him to help you move ahead.

—Dave Egner

Fact of Nature

The Tahquamenon River area is the main setting for Henry Wadsworth Longfellow's epic poem *The Song of Hiawatha.*

✳ COMPASS POINT

Move ahead in Jesus' name.

Hope for the Helpless

Guidebook Reading: Luke 15:1–7

And when he comes home, he calls together his friends and neighbors, saying to them, "Rejoice with me, for I have found my sheep which was lost!" —LUKE 15:6

We can be delivered from our sins only after realizing how helpless we are. At that point God can move into our life with saving power—but not before!

Nineteenth-century Scottish pastor Andrew Bonar said that in the highlands of Scotland, sheep occasionally wander off among the rocky crags and get themselves trapped on dangerous ledges. Attracted by the sweet grass on the mountainside, they leap down ten to twelve feet to get to it. But they can't get back up. A shepherd will allow the helpless animal to remain there for days until it becomes so weak it's unable to stand up. Finally, he ties a rope around his waist and goes over the cliff to the rocky shelf and rescues the one that has strayed.

Someone asked Bonar, "Why doesn't the shepherd go down right away?"

"Ah," came the reply, "sheep are so foolish that they would dash right over the precipice and be killed if the herdsman didn't wait until their strength was nearly gone."

How like human nature! Man tries to gain salvation by his own efforts. During my pastoral ministry, I often stood at the bedsides of desperate people who only months before had spurned the grace of God. They had tried to make themselves acceptable to Him by improving their lives. Not until they were helpless did they realize that they couldn't escape from the "ledge of no return." Then they were ready to accept help from the Good Shepherd.

It's impossible to get to heaven on your own. But there is hope the moment you admit you are helpless. If you're at that point right now, Christ is waiting to save you. Trust Him today!

—*Paul Van Gorder*

> ## Fact *of* Nature
>
> There are more sheep in Scotland than there are people: 7.4 million sheep, 5.2 million people.

 COMPASS POINT

Jesus saves those who know they need saving.

Deceit and a Smart Dog

Guidebook Reading: Proverbs 14:1–8

Bread gained by deceit is sweet to a man, but afterward his mouth will be filled with gravel. —PROVERBS 20:17

An elderly woman had been invited by some friends to enjoy the cool breezes and quiet atmosphere of their summer cottage. The owners, however, had a very large spoiled dog. The houseguest had been given freedom to use the place, and she frequently occupied a large armchair that she found most restful. But, alas, she soon discovered it was also the spot where the owner's pet liked to relax. Being afraid of the animal, she never dared to command him to get out of the comfortable chair, but instead she would go to the window and call out, "Look, Rover, cats! CATS!" The dog would rush over to the window and bark furiously while she slipped quietly into the vacant seat.

One day Rover entered the room and found that the guest had beaten him to his choice resting place. Racing to the window and looking out, he suddenly acted very excited. Howling and barking ferociously, he began to scratch the walls with his front paws. When the woman hurried to the window to see what was the matter, the dog seized the opportunity to jump into the empty chair. Apparently he had caught on to her trick!

It just goes to show: Deceit practiced on others will often be paid back in kind.

Are you guilty of cheating, lying, or engaging in questionable business deals? If so, be aware that there are two problems with that. First, God frowns on such actions, and second, sooner or later people will get wise to you. When they do, the outcome will be as unpleasant as biting down on a mouthful of stones (Proverbs 20:17).

Beware of deceit; it always backfires!

—*Henry Bosch*

Fact of Nature

According to a study done by Oxford University researchers and published in the *Proceedings of the National Academy of Sciences* journal, dogs are smarter than cats. Feel free to disagree.

 COMPASS POINT

Living in deceit is a joyless existence.

Making Tracks

Guidebook Reading: Colossians 1:9–14

For you were once darkness, but now you are light in the Lord. Walk as children of light. —EPHESIANS 5:8

When we were boys, my brother Marvin and I would often go hiking. Early in the morning after a fresh snowfall we would tramp through the fields looking for the tracks of animals that had been on the prowl during the night. We found great satisfaction in identifying their trails. In addition to the prints of rabbits, pheasants, field mice, possums, skunks, and even an occasional deer, we would also see the crisscrossing tracks of our bulldog Mike, indicating that he had been doing some investigating on his own. I was always impressed by the fact that each animal had its own distinct "walk," which immediately identified it.

Fact *of* Nature

Dogs' tracks are sloppy and indicate little pattern. Cat tracks, though, look like a dotted line since they carefully place their hind feet on top of the prints made by their front feet. Foxes make marks similar to the ones cats make. This is called "direct register."

Similarly, our walk as believers should be an identifying mark. Romans 6:4 tells us that "we . . . should walk in newness of life." In Romans 13:13 we read, "Let us walk properly . . . not in lewdness and lust, not in strife and envy." Ephesians 4:17 admonishes us not to "walk as the rest of the Gentiles walk, in the futility of their mind." And Ephesians 5:15 exhorts us to "walk circumspectly."

Members of the kingdom of God are often more inconsistent in their walk than creatures of the animal kingdom. Whereas a bear or deer always reveals his true identity by the tracks he leaves, a Christian's walk sometimes belies his true nature. What does your conduct tell others about you? Does it identify you as a child of God? The apostle John tells us, "If we say that we have fellowship with Him, and walk in darkness, we lie" (1 John 1:6).

What do the "tracks" you leave behind tell others about you?

—*Richard DeHaan*

 COMPASS POINT

Do you leave evidence of your faith with those around you?

First Pride—Then the Fall

Guidebook Reading: Luke 18:9–14

Pride goes before destruction, and a haughty spirit before a fall. —Proverbs 16:18

I was canoeing down Michigan's Pine River with my fourteen-year-old friend Kim. I was the speaker for the teenage division of a summer Bible camp, and she and I were assigned to the same canoe. The river was high; the way was filled with rocks, fallen logs, and trees that had come down in a recent storm. It took hard work to paddle through the strong current and tricky turns, and to avoid the overhangs and logs.

When we would do well for fifty or a hundred yards, I would say, "Hey, we're getting good at this!" Kim would reply, "Pride goes before a fall!" She was right. The next thing we knew we would be plowing into the bank, scraping over a rock, or ducking under some overhanging branches. And we went into the chilly waters of the river more than once!

It seems to happen every time. As soon as we begin to think we are really good at something or that we have made some great achievement—as soon as we take pride in it—something humbling occurs to bring us "back down to earth." The more pride we have in ourselves and the greater we consider our achievement to be, the more certain will be the reminder that we have "feet of clay."

This truth is clearly set forth in Proverbs 16:18. Those who boast will be brought down. Those who exalt themselves will be humbled. If you start to feel boastful, be careful. Pride leads to destruction, and a haughty spirit will make you fall.

—*Dave Egner*

> ## Fact *of* Nature
>
> The scenic Pine River watershed is the former home of Ottawa, Potawatomi, and Chippewa Indians. There are nearly 100 archaeological sites along the watershed.

✳ COMPASS POINT

Humility looks good on you.

Learning from the Redwoods

Guidebook Reading: Isaiah 65:17–66:2

As the days of a tree, so shall be the days of My people. —ISAIAH 65:22

North America's Pacific Coast Redwoods are some of the biggest trees in the world. The tallest on record, Hyperion, soars 379 feet into the air.

During a visit to California's Muir Woods National Park, I was surprised and overwhelmed by the enormity of the redwoods. Trees as tall as a thirty-story building seemed to press me into the forest floor while drawing my thoughts upward.

The memory of what I felt at the base of some of the tallest and oldest trees in the world has left me with lingering thoughts about their origin. Those redwoods, like the family tree of our own humanity, are rooted in a Creator who is infinitely and eternally greater than His creation.

The prophet Isaiah caught a glimpse of this God. In a vision that mingled the wonders of a messianic kingdom with the promise of a new heaven and earth, he describes One who makes the skies His throne and the earth His footstool (Isaiah 66:1).

Yet Isaiah saw something even more overwhelming. He saw a great God who wants His people to "be glad and rejoice forever in what I create" (65:18). In response, let's bow before Him in humble adoration (66:2).

—*Mart DeHaan*

Fact *of* Nature

Hyperion, by most reckoning, is between 700 and 800 years old. If it is around 800 years old, it would have just been getting its first roots down during the time of the signing of the Magna Carta in England in 1215.

✸ COMPASS POINT

If God can create a tree, surely we can worship Him for it.

Of Birds and Stars

Guidebook Reading: Job 12:1–9

But now ask the beasts, and they will teach you; and the birds of the air, and they will tell you. —JOB 12:7

Nature teaches us much about God. For one thing, it shows His kindness in providing animals and birds with inborn impulses and patterns that aid them in adjusting to what is often a hostile environment. Their lives are thus guided and preserved despite their limited intelligence. For instance, some birds would die if they had to stay all year in areas of extremely cold weather. Therefore the Lord has graciously given them migrating instincts.

Take, for instance, the small indigo bunting (a member of the finch family). This little guy apparently steers his way 2,000 miles south every year just by looking over his shoulder at the northern sky! This night-flying bird does not seem to rely on any one star or constellation for his direction, says Stephen T. Emlen of Cornell University. Rather, this bird recognizes the whole geometrical pattern of the skies within 35 degrees of the North Star, and it can be confused only when that part of the sky is entirely blocked off by clouds. The bunting then wisely discontinues flight until it can once again get a clear view of the configuration made by the northern star groups.

> ## Fact *of* Nature
>
> The indigo bunting, a brilliantly blue bird, winters in the Caribbean islands and in Central America.

The prophet Jeremiah tells us that the Lord gave these "ordinances of the moon and the stars for a light by night" (Jeremiah 31:35). Apparently, the nighttime lights not only aid people in navigation but they also assist our feathered friends, the birds.

Observing nature, so crammed with beauty, wonder, and design, we can see through the lives of the beasts and the fowls of the air that there is a gracious heavenly Father who provides for His creatures in wisdom. This in turn should call forth our adoration and praise!

—*Henry Bosch*

✹ COMPASS POINT

Observe nature and you'll find God.

The Spring That Satisfies

Guidebook Reading: John 4:1–14

Both the singers and the players of the instruments say, "All my springs are in you."
—Psalm 87:7

When the pump stopped working at our family cabin in Michigan's Upper Peninsula, our friend Lottie Kaulfield brought us several jugs of wonderful-tasting fresh water.

"Is this from your well?" I asked. She said no, and then she told me she had stopped at a fresh-flowing spring just south of the little village of Paradise. The next time I drove into that town, I located the spring by the roadside and saw a group of bikers drinking from it. On my return, I noticed two backpackers resting beside it. No one knows how many weary travelers have had their thirst quenched by the cool, refreshing water from that spring.

The psalmist said of God, "All my springs are in you." Commenting on this verse in the devotional book *Daily Remembrances*, James Smith said:

> *Jesus is the fountain of living waters; the wells of salvation are found in His person, work, and word. He says, "If anyone thirsts, let him come to Me and drink." The springs of comfort, peace, and salvation are all in Him, and in Him for us; therefore, [they are] called our springs. The waters cleanse from all defilement, refresh the faint and weary, and satisfy the longing soul. The springs bespeak plenitude—whosoever will may come and take, for they are never dry. We are absolutely dependent on Jesus . . . Our desires should concentrate in Him.*

Yes, as pilgrim saints, all our "springs" are in Jesus. Why then should we look to any other source for spiritual refreshment and renewal? Let every Christian come to Him expectantly and often. He satisfies the thirsting soul.

—Dave Egner

Fact *of* Nature

One of the largest freshwater springs in the world is called Big Spring, and it is located in Missouri. It discharges an average of 276 million gallons of water a day.

✴ COMPASS POINT

Jesus alone can quench your spiritual thirst.

When the Star Falls

Guidebook Reading: Revelation 8:1–13

Then the third angel sounded: And a great star fell from heaven.
—Revelation 8:10

Scientists have suggested that one of the largest stellar systems in our galaxy is about to self-destruct. Eta Carinae, a binary system that has a mass 100 times greater than that of our sun, is giving signs that its life is about over. Researchers say that it could become a supernova—a blazing, exploding star system—in the next several thousand years. What is especially interesting about the report is the idea that since light from Eta Carinae takes 8,000 years to reach the earth, the actual explosion could have already taken place.

This striking fact reminds me of the nature of biblical prophecy. For example, the predictions found in Revelation 8 are often written in the past tense. This is done because even though the prophet is writing of a future event, he has already "seen" it. Also, in the mind of God it's as if the events have already happened.

Even though Christians differ on the interpretation of Revelation 8, we can definitely say that God's judgment against sin is certain. The outpouring of His anger against those who continually resist Him is so sure that it has been written about in the past tense. This should cause us to reflect with the apostle Peter, who wrote so appropriately, "Therefore, since all these things will be dissolved, what manner of persons ought you to be in holy conduct and godliness?" (2 Peter 3:11).

As Christians, we know what's ahead for this world, and that knowledge should keep us living close to God.

—*Mart DeHaan*

Fact *of* Nature

Eta Carinae was thought to be a single star until 2005 when a NASA satellite telescope detected that it had a partner, indicating that it is in a binary system.

 Compass Point

Judgment is coming; stay close to Jesus.

Who–or What–Do We Thank?

Guidebook Reading: Psalm 100

Enter into His gates with thanksgiving, and into His courts with praise. Be thankful to Him, and bless His name. —Psalm 100:4

On my way to work one day I saw a bumper sticker that read, "Did you thank a green plant today?" That question was so striking that I wondered what was in the mind of the one who wrote it. Plants, of course, are essential to the balance of nature, for by the process of photosynthesis they liberate oxygen from water. Plants are also a source of food, fuel, drugs, building materials, and industrial products. Was the bumper sticker suggesting that because we are so dependent upon plants we should thank them for maintaining life on our planet? If that's what the originator was thinking, he or she certainly had a lot to learn about who should receive our gratitude.

Nature bears marvelous testimony to the wisdom of the Creator. The interdependence of one life form upon another makes us realize that we are part of a wonderful, complex system that is characterized by beauty, harmony, and balance. But to thank a plant for this reminds me of Paul's description of people who "worshiped and served the creature rather than the Creator" (Romans 1:25). God alone is worthy of our gratitude! He set our world in motion, and He sustains it by His power.

> ## Fact *of* Nature
>
> Green plants are the only plants that make food and produce oxygen. They do this through the process of photosynthesis.

Yes, it's wonderful to be alive! And indeed deep feelings of appreciation often well up within us. Yet we must always direct our praise to the One who not only gives us the air we breathe but who also imparts eternal life through faith in Christ.

I would like to see that bumper sticker changed to read, "Did you thank God today?"

—*Dennis DeHaan*

✦ COMPASS POINT

Praise God today for the things He created.

Open Wide

Guidebook Reading: Psalm 81

I am the LORD your God, who brought you out of the land of Egypt; open your mouth wide, and I will fill it. —PSALM 81:10

As a boy, I was always thrilled to discover a newly constructed robin's nest. It was fascinating to watch for the eggs and then to wait for those featherless little creatures with bulging eyes and gaping mouths to break out of their shells. Standing at a distance, I could see their heads bobbing unsteadily and their mouths yawning wide open—inviting mother robin to give them their dinner.

As I recalled those childhood scenes, I thought of God's promise: "I am the LORD your God . . . open your mouth wide, and I will fill it" (Psalm 81:10). In spite of this gracious offer to Israel, the people ignored God, and He "gave them over to their own stubborn heart, to walk in their own counsels" (v. 12). If they had accepted God's offer, "He would have fed them also with the finest of wheat; and with honey from the rock" (v. 16).

God longs to give us spiritual food. And He will satisfy our spiritual hunger as we study His Word, worship with others, listen to faithful Bible teachers, read literature with good spiritual content, and daily depend on Him.

If we refuse God's provisions, we will suffer spiritual malnutrition and fail to grow. But if we open our mouth wide, be assured, God will fill it.

—*Richard DeHaan*

> ## Fact *of* Nature
>
> Robins don't live long. The average lifespan of an American robin is two years. Many of them die before they reach one year of age.

✳ COMPASS POINT

Let God feed your soul.

The Hidden Rattler

Guidebook Reading: 2 Kings 20:12–21

There is nothing among my treasures that I have not shown them. —2 KINGS 20:15

When I was a boy, our family lived on a farm where, during one brief period in the springtime, we killed thirteen rattlesnakes. Actually, a rattler can be easily destroyed if one knows where he is and how far he can reach when he strikes. Therefore, my brothers and I never worried about the snakes we could see. However, we were genuinely concerned about stepping on one whose presence we had not detected.

King Hezekiah, spoken of in 2 Kings 20, was thus subtly "bitten" by a hidden temptation rather than being seduced by a gross and obvious evil. He allowed a measure of pride and undue self-reliance to blight his career. He should have put his full trust in the Lord for protection from his enemies, but instead he sought safety by an alliance with idolatrous men. He welcomed a delegation from Babylon and showed them all his wealth to prove that Judah would be a valuable ally (2 Chronicles 32:25, 31). His action displeased the Lord, and as a result the prophet Isaiah was sent to announce coming judgment.

Sadly, this otherwise good king marred his reign by this sin. Although it was not an act of gross immorality or extreme cruelty, it nevertheless grieved God. The warning for us? We need to be on guard lest we allow pride and self-confidence to build up in our hearts until we, like Hezekiah, succumb to the wiles of the Enemy.

Fact of Nature

It has been estimated that between 7,000 and 8,000 people are bitten by rattlesnakes in the United States each year. On average, just five of those injuries are fatal in any single year.

You may have prepared yourself to stand against gross invitations to sin that would besmirch your name, but you may not be ready for life's subtle temptations. Beware of "hidden rattlers." They are usually the most dangerous of all!

—*Herb Vander Lugt*

 COMPASS POINT

Beware of sneaky sins.

Bound to Be Free

Guidebook Reading: John 8:31–45

For he who is called in the Lord while a slave is the Lord's freedman. Likewise he who is called while free is Christ's slave. —1 CORINTHIANS 7:22

The image of a duck flying through the air with an arrow embedded in her body is still fresh in my memory. I saw the picture in a local newspaper that carried the story of a mallard duck that had eluded the attempts of rescuers to capture her and remove the foreign object.

A couple of months later a Canada goose flew into Wisconsin with the same problem. A young bow hunter had hit his mark, but that didn't stop this bird. She evaded game wardens, avoided tranquilizer-laced grain, and even dodged cannon-fired nets. Finally, after about a month, the wound seemed to exhaust the goose, and she was caught with a fishing net. Surgery was performed, and it wasn't long until she was returned to freedom. If geese could think, I'm sure she would have wondered why in the world she had tried so hard to elude her captors for so long.

> ## Fact of Nature
>
> Population estimates of ducks in the US indicate that Americans share the land with somewhere around 42 million of these winged creatures.

The experience of these reluctant captives reminds me of the men Christ spoke to in John 8. They too were slow to realize the seriousness of their condition. They didn't understand the motives of the One who, to them, looked like a captor. After all, He wanted them to surrender the ultimate direction of their lives to His Spirit. He asked them to become His disciples. He implored them to become spiritual bond-slaves. But they were unable to realize that by surrendering they could "be made free" (v. 33).

Is it possible we have forgotten that real freedom is found only in being secure in Christ? This relates not only to our ultimate salvation but also to our daily walk with the Lord. As servants of Christ, we are bound to be free.

—*Mart DeHaan*

✳ COMPASS POINT

True freedom comes in being redeemed by Jesus.

"Bee" Happy?

Guidebook Reading: Ecclesiastes 2:1–11

For men will be lovers of themselves . . . lovers of pleasure rather than lovers of God.
—2 TIMOTHY 3:2, 4

Did you hear about the overindulgent bee? This little buzzer found a pot of honey and thought partaking of it would be a fine way to save all the trouble of flying about the meadows to gather the sweetness little by little out of the cups of flowers. Oblivious to all else, the tiny creature therefore began to sip out of that luscious dish of nectar, reveling in its delights. But when she began to get tired and satiated, she found—poor bee—that her wings were all clogged and would not open, nor could she drag her body out of the sticky mass. And so eventually she died, buried in pleasure!

For human beings, the problem is similar. A constant search for worldly enjoyment destroys the love and sense of God in the soul. Indeed, a life made up chiefly of pleasure is usually poor and worthless in the sight of the Lord. Writing under the Holy Spirit's inspiration, Timothy says that "in the last days," people will be more concerned with the pleasures of this world than the true joys of the matchless love of God.

> ## Fact *of* Nature
>
> In a lifetime, a honeybee will produce a grand total of 1/12th of a teaspoon of honey.

We have but to look around us to see what this maddening search for thrills has brought as far as sorrow and shipwrecked lives are concerned. The "pleasures of sin" are "passing" (Hebrews 11:25) and will leave one with a bitter taste and eventually a ruined life. On the other hand, the joys of Christ are sweet, having promise for this life as well as for the one that is to come.

Many will find destruction in overindulgence and continual thrill seeking. Make sure you are not one of them.

—*Henry Bosch*

✳ COMPASS POINT

Life comes from trusting Jesus, not from seeking pleasure.

What's with the Loons?

Guidebook Reading: 2 Corinthians 12:1–10

Time would fail me to tell of Gideon and Barak . . . who through faith subdued kingdoms . . . [and] out of weakness were made strong. —Hebrews 11:32–34

I'm always amused when I watch the loons lift into flight off Piatt Lake in Michigan's Upper Peninsula. They half-run, half-flap across the water for hundreds of feet before getting enough speed to lift into the air. I wondered why until I learned that, unlike most birds, loons have solid bones. Their added weight makes it difficult for them to get airborne.

I also learned that loons are clumsy on land because their legs are set farther back on their bodies than other birds. Walking is so difficult that many loons simply scoot across land to their nesting places. But these disadvantages—heavy bones, legs set far back—are also tremendous advantages. Because of their weight and leg placement, loons can dive deeper, farther, and faster. This is essential for catching fish and escaping predators.

Fact *of* Nature

Although a common Great Lakes loon weighs only about 10 pounds, it needs to eat about 2 pounds of fish a day to survive.

What we see as disadvantages in our lives can be turned into advantages, and apparent weaknesses can be transformed into strengths. That was true of the apostle Paul, whose "thorn in the flesh" became an opportunity for God's strength to be seen in his weakness (2 Corinthians 12:7–9).

Is a weakness holding you down? Is it shyness or a physical limitation? Ask God to turn it into a strength for His glory.

—*Dave Egner*

✳ COMPASS POINT

God turns our feebleness into His power.

Flying Backward

Guidebook Reading: Psalm 139:7–16

I will praise You, for I am fearfully and wonderfully made. —PSALM 139:14

I had read that hummingbirds can fly backward, but the cynic in me doubted it. So when my wife mounted a hummingbird feeder by the kitchen window and filled it with sugar water, I sat down with a cup of coffee to see if it was true.

Before long, hummingbirds began to appear—a ruby-throated male and several females. I soon gave up trying to watch their wings as they flew. All I could see was a blur. I was captivated by the feisty little creatures as they darted up and down, away and back, vying for an open spot at the feeder and chasing one another away.

After a while, only one bird was left—her long, thin beak sucking up the liquid. Then, when she was finished, she flew straight backward, then up, and finally darted out of sight among the trees.

How did she do it? God knows. Sometime on the fifth day of creation, while He was forming whales, sharks, orioles, and loons, God created the hummingbird with its amazing ability to fly backward—a miracle of His power.

I didn't need that awesome illustration to prove the existence and brilliance of God. But it did remind me once again that I have every reason to worship God, for I too am "fearfully and wonderfully made" (Psalm 139:14).

—*Dave Egner*

Fact *of* Nature

Some perennials that attract hummingbirds: columbine, hosta, yucca, coral bells, cardinal flower, lupine, foxglove, and bee balm.

✳ COMPASS POINT

Sometimes it's the little things that remind us what a big God we serve.

He Can Be Trusted

Guidebook Reading: Psalm 84

O LORD of hosts, blessed is the man who trusts in You. —PSALM 84:12

I was sitting in my chair by the window, staring out through fir and spruce trees to the mountains beyond, lost in thought. I looked down and saw a young fox, staring up at my face. She was as still as a stone.

Days before, I had seen her at the edge of the woods, looking nervously over her shoulder at me. I went to the kitchen for an egg and rolled it toward the place I had last seen her. Each day I put another egg on the lawn, and each day she ventured out of the trees just long enough to pick it up. Then she would dart back into the woods.

Now she had come on her own to my door to get an egg, convinced, I suppose, that I meant her no harm.

This incident reminded my wife of David's invitation: "Oh, taste and see that the LORD is good" (Psalm 34:8). How do we start doing that? By taking in His Word. As we read and reflect on His compassion and lovingkindness, we learn that He can be trusted (84:12). We lose our dread of getting closer to Him. Our fear becomes a healthy respect and honor of Him.

You may at times distrust God, as the fox was wary of me at first. But give Him a chance to prove His love. Read about Jesus in the Gospels. Read the praises to God in the Psalms. Taste and see that He is good!

Fact of Nature

A man in Derby, England, used patience and quite a bit of ham to train a wild fox to stand on his hind legs and beg for food. Animal experts were amazed that this was even possible.

—*David Roper*

✳ COMPASS POINT

How close you get to God depends on how much you trust Him.

Ants, Antifreeze, and Adoration

Guidebook Reading: Psalm 104:16–24

O LORD, how manifold are Your works! In wisdom, You have made them all.
—PSALM 104:24

God speaks to us through His special revelation, the Bible, but also through His general revelation as it is demonstrated in creation.

Some years ago I was sent a *Time* magazine article that made some interesting observations about black carpenter ants. Apparently, these little insects have the ability to manufacture "antifreeze" in their bodies to preserve their lives during the cold months of the year. Biochemist Fred Smith of the University of Minnesota was quoted as saying that they actually make glycerol, a chemical that closely resembles the substance we use to protect our car engines from the frigid blasts of winter. Since the active summer larvae of these creatures do not contain this ingredient, Smith reasoned that the ants must have a mechanism that reacts to cold to produce this protective "alcohol." Hibernating black carpenter ants proved to have as much as 10 percent of this antifreeze in their bodies, but when they were gradually warmed up and became active, all of it disappeared.

> **Fact *of* Nature**
>
> Carpenter ants produce the glycerol in their bodies when the temperature reaches a certain low point. This inactive phase of their winter existence is called diapause.

Logic would seem to indicate that these defenses could not have developed over a long period of time—otherwise the first colony of insects would have been frozen to death. It would seem more reasonable that our creator God endowed these little creatures with a built-in antifreeze mechanism.

As we delve into the intricate and marvelous designs in nature, which have been masterminded by God, we exclaim with the psalmist, "O LORD, how manifold are Your works! In wisdom You have made them all!" Yes, ants, antifreeze, and adoration are clearly interrelated!

—*Henry Bosch*

✳ COMPASS POINT

God's creation should lead us to worship.

The Right View of Jesus

Guidebook Reading: Matthew 16:13–17

Simon Peter answered and said, "You are the Christ, the Son of the living God."
—MATTHEW 16:16

What we believe about Christ determines how we respond to Him. If we do not recognize Him as the Son of God, it is unlikely that we'll give Him the honor and devotion He deserves.

I thought of this truth after reading the story of an unusual-looking rock that was discovered in a stream in North Carolina in 1799. Not knowing its worth, the boy who found it took it home, where it was used as a doorstop for several years. Finally, the homeowner took it to town where he sold it for $3.50. When he subsequently discovered that it was gold—and that the buyer had sold it for $3,500—he recouped some of his money. Then he began looking for more gold in his creek and eventually became a wealthy gold miner. That ignored doorstop turned out to be the biggest gold nugget ever found east of the Rockies.

When Christ appeared on the earth, many people failed to recognize His true identity. Some folks thought of Him as only a Galilean peasant and dismissed Him from their minds. Many others admired Him as a great teacher, but they did not follow Him. They were like the young man in the story who saw only a doorstop in the priceless nugget that had been found in the river. On the other hand, Peter clearly saw Jesus as the promised Son of God. And what a difference it made in his response! Because he had the right view of the Savior, he yielded his life completely to Him.

Can you, like the apostle, say of Jesus, "You are the Christ, the Son of the living God"?

—*Paul Van Gorder*

Fact of Nature

The East Rand Gold Mine in Boksburg, South Africa, is among the world's deepest gold mines. It extends to a depth of 11,762 feet. The temperature of the rocks at that depth is 300 degrees Fahrenheit.

✳ COMPASS POINT

Do you recognize Jesus for who He is?

The God of the Beautiful

Guidebook Reading: Isaiah 33:13–17

He has made everything beautiful in its time. —ECCLESIASTES 3:11

A brand-new Christian, gazing upon a sunset for the first time after his spiritual eyes were opened, exclaimed, "What a beautiful world our Lord has made!"

God is indeed a God of beauty! Breathtaking is the splendor of the sunrise, the rainbow, the majestic mountains, the fertile fields, the delicate clouds, the stately trees, and the many multicolored flowers.

Just outside my study window grows a flower garden, each of the blossoms containing a sermon, each petal a song, and all together producing a symphony of praise to God.

Some flowers, however, blossom unseen by human eyes. Eighteenth-century British poet Thomas Gray penned the following lines in his famous "Elegy Written in a Country Churchyard."

> *Full many a flower is born to blush unseen,*
> *And waste its sweetness on the desert air.*

I must say respectfully to Mr. Gray that even such blossoms of which he speaks are not wasted, for they attract the insects and thereby pollinate their neighbors, thus preventing extinction of the species. Neither is their fragrance lost upon the desert air, for the honeybee attracted by the perfume—that mysterious means of communication—flies for miles to gather a bit of its nectar. There is no waste in God's economy. There is a place for beauty in life, and unhappy is the person who fails to see it.

We can learn a lesson from the little, unnoticed flower. Even though you may feel unimportant and neglected, God has a high purpose for your life! Keep beautiful, fragrant, and attractive spiritually for His glory! Praise Him for the marvels of nature and the wonders of grace.

—M. R. DeHaan

Fact *of* Nature

Even in the dead of winter an inhabited honeybee hive maintains an inner temperature of 93 degrees Fahrenheit.

 COMPASS POINT

God has a purpose for you: Proclaim His glory.

Stay in the Light

Guidebook Reading: Romans 13:8–14

The night is far spent, the day is at hand. Therefore let us cast off the works of darkness, and let us put on the armor of light. —ROMANS 13:12

On an overcast night deep in Michigan's Upper Peninsula, it becomes extremely dark in the woods. While staying at our cabin in the U.P., my family and I notice that when we first step outside at night we can't see a thing. After a little while, however, our eyes grow accustomed to the darkness. Soon we can distinguish shapes, and before long we are able to follow the path down to the lake. When we have been away from the light long enough, we begin to feel at home in the blackness. But that could be dangerous, because we still can't see everything that might be lurking in the shadows.

I'm sure you see the spiritual parallel. When we've been saved awhile, we are comfortable in the light. Occasionally, however, we are tempted to go back into the worldly way of darkness. But because we are used to the light, we can't see in the dark— so we quickly return. If we don't, we face a subtle danger. If we stay in the darkness of sin for very long, it doesn't really seem so bad anymore. What began as a brief exposure to the absence of light soon becomes a familiar way of living. And we all know how much danger lurks there.

Jesus, who is the light of the world, came to this sinful earth to overcome spiritual darkness by giving light from above to all who receive Him as Savior. When we become His followers, we should "have no fellowship with the unfruitful works of darkness" (Ephesians 5:11).

Don't flirt with danger by walking down a path that leads to darkness. You'll find the going much safer if you stay in the light of Jesus.

—*Dave Egner*

Fact *of* Nature

Galloway Forest Park in Scotland is one of the darkest spots on earth because of the dense forest, the distance from major cities, and the rain-cleansing atmosphere.

✴ COMPASS POINT

Avoid the dangers of darkness.

Tough Trees

Guidebook Reading: Romans 5:1–5

Tribulation produces perseverance; and perseverance, character; and character, hope.
—ROMANS 5:3–4

Bristlecone pines are the world's oldest living trees. Several are estimated to be 3,000 to 4,000 years old. In 1957, scientist Edmund Schulman found one he named "Methuselah." This ancient, gnarled pine is nearly 5,000 years old! It was an old tree when the Egyptians were building the pyramids.

Bristlecones grow atop the mountains of the western United States at elevations of 10,000 to 11,000 feet. They've been able to survive some of the harshest living conditions on earth: arctic temperatures, fierce winds, thin air, and little rainfall.

Their brutal environment is actually one of the reasons they've survived for millennia. Hardship has produced extraordinary strength and staying power.

Paul taught that "tribulation produces . . . character" (Romans 5:3–4). Adversity is part of the process God uses to produce good results in our lives. Trouble, if it turns us to the Lord, could actually be the best thing for us. It leaves us wholly dependent on Him.

So we should pray not just for relief from our affliction, but also for the grace to turn it into greater openness to God and to His will for us. Then we can be strong in calamity and at peace in the place where God has planted us.

—*David Roper*

Fact of Nature

Scientists believe Methuselah is 4,843 years old (in 2012). If that is true, the tree was already ancient when Moses led the Israelites through the desert toward the Promised Land. Methuselah is located in eastern California.

✶ COMPASS POINT

The trouble God allows is there to make us stronger and more trusting.

New Songs

Guidebook Reading: Psalm 40:1–10

He has put a new song in my mouth—praise to our God. —Psalm 40:3

The song of the humpback whale is one of the strangest in nature. It is a weird combination of high- and low-pitched groanings. Those who have studied the humpback whale say their songs are noteworthy because these giants of the deep are continually changing them. New patterns are added and old ones eliminated, so over a period of time the whale actually sings a whole new song.

There's a sense in which a Christian should be continually composing new songs of praise around the fresh mercies of God. Unfortunately, many of us just keep singing "the same old song."

Certainly we must repeatedly affirm the fundamentals of our faith. But, as the psalmist tells us, the works of God's deliverance in the lives of His people are many. His works, which are more than we can count, give us reasons to express our praise to Him in numerous ways (Psalm 40:5).

So why do we express our testimony of God's saving grace in the same old way year after year? A fresh experience of the mercies of the cross and of Christ's resurrection power should continually fill our hearts and minds with new songs.

The gospel story never changes—thank God for that. But our songs of praise should be ever new.

—*Mart DeHaan*

Fact of Nature

One website that provides whale songs for you to listen to is www.oceanmammalinst.com/songs.

✸ Compass Point

Has anything new happened for which you can praise God?

Stop the Slide

Guidebook Reading: Isaiah 1:7–17

Wash yourselves, make yourselves clean; put away the evil of your doings from before My eyes. Cease to do evil. —ISAIAH 1:16

The *Rocky Mountain News* carried a story about three climbers who were traversing from Colorado's Brainard Lake across Pawnee Pass when they lost the trail in the snow. The climbers had some critical choices to make. Unfortunately, they did almost everything wrong.

First, they chose to keep on going. Then, when they saw Crater Lake far below, with a gentle slope of snow heading down toward it, they decided to slide down toward the lake, hoping they would find the trail again. They started slowly, but the slope got steeper and steeper. Soon they were hurtling down. Then they heard water. The slope was heading toward a waterfall! In desperation they dug in their heels, slowing their rapid descent. Fortunately, they stopped their slide before it was too late and managed to inch their way to a ledge to await rescue.

> ## Fact *of* Nature
>
> Colorado's Crater Lake is situated at more than 10,000 feet above sea level. The waterfall mentioned here is on the south end of the lake.

The progressive nature of sin follows much the same course. First we lose our way and begin a downward slide—slowly at first. Then, before we realize it, we're hurtling downward, out of control and in great spiritual danger.

Like those climbers, we have to do everything we can to stop our slide. Isaiah said it well: "Cease to do evil" (1:16). Don't keep going. Stop the slide!

—Dave Egner

✸ COMPASS POINT

Avoid sin's downward pull.

A Life-and-Death Matter

Guidebook Reading: Romans 8:12–18

If you live according to the flesh you will die; but if by the Spirit you put to death the deeds of the body, you will live. —ROMANS 8:13

Nature is violent. Life and death are the law of field, stream, and jungle. A lion stalks a gazelle. A heron stands motionless at the edge of a pond, its long, sharp beak poised and ready to kill. High overhead a red-tailed hawk holds its deadly talons close to its body, watching for movement in the grass below. Suddenly a rabbit's pain becomes an eagle's gain. A leopard family exists at a zebra's expense. Each survives on another's demise. This sounds natural enough. But it's more graphic than most of us care to watch.

The principle that nothing lives unless something else dies extends beyond nature to our daily walk with God. Interests of the flesh must succumb to the interests of the Spirit, or the interests of the Spirit will succumb to the interests of the flesh. In the jungles and fields and streams of our own heart, something must always die so that something else can live.

We can't be committed to Christ and to the world at the same time. We can't be filled with His Spirit if we are protecting the life of selfish interests. That's why our Lord said so pointedly that we will need to die daily to our own selves if we are going to walk with Him (Luke 9:23, 24). We must continually choose. What will die so that He can live freely in us?

—*Mart DeHaan*

Fact *of* Nature

Animal Planet lists the Top Five Predators in this order:
1. Shark
2. Lion
3. Grizzly Bear
4. Killer Whale
5. Crocodile

✳ COMPASS POINT

To walk with Jesus, die daily.

The High Cost of Getting Even

Guidebook Reading: Esther 3:1–6; 7:1–6, 10

So they hanged Haman on the gallows that he had prepared for Mordecai.
—ESTHER 7:10

A group of people touring Yellowstone National Park watched a grizzly bear eating some food that had been set out for him by the attendants. Suddenly a skunk appeared on the scene and boldly began to steal some of the rations. Since the sightseers had been told that all of the animals in the park were afraid of the huge beast, they asked how this little creature dared to get so close. Their guide replied, "Oh, the bear is disturbed by it and would like to take out his vengeance on the impudent skunk, but he knows the high cost of getting even!" Anyone who has lived on a farm and smelled a hapless dog that made the mistake of attacking this striped member of the weasel family knows the results of such folly.

Esther 7 tells the sad story of Haman, an important official in the Persian government. He was angry because Mordecai refused to bow before him, and he determined to gain revenge by having this God-fearing Jew hanged and the entire Hebrew nation exterminated. The Lord intervened, however, foiling the plans of this cruel, vindictive man, and bringing about his execution on the very gallows he had prepared for his enemy. Yes, Haman paid the high cost of getting even!

> ### Fact of Nature
>
> Making a skunk a pet means de-scenting the little critter. Some people disagree with this practice because it robs the skunk of its defense mechanism should it escape into the wild.

The Bible declares, "'Vengeance is mine; I will repay,' says the Lord" (Romans 12:19), and the person whose heart is filled with hatred will learn that he can't harbor thoughts of retaliation without suffering for it. Such an attitude will mar one's personality, impair one's physical health, and disrupt his fellowship with God. In many ways he will discover the high cost of getting even.

—*Herb Vander Lugt*

✳ COMPASS POINT

If you live with the desire to get even, you'll be robbing yourself of victory and joy.

Shark Tonic

Guidebook Reading: Hebrews 12:1–11

Let us lay aside every weight, and the sin which so easily ensnares us, and let us run with endurance the race that is set before us. — HEBREWS 12:1

Have you ever heard of shark "tonic"? It isn't a serum that prevents shark attacks or a medicine given to sharks. The actual term is "tonic immobility," described as "a natural state of paralysis that animals enter . . . Sharks can be placed in a tonic immobility state by turning them upside down. The shark remains in this state of paralysis for an average of fifteen minutes before it recovers."

Imagine that—a dangerous shark can be made vulnerable simply by turning it upside down. The state of tonic immobility makes the shark incapable of movement.

Sin is like that. Our ability to honor our Lord, for which we are created in Christ, can be put into "tonic immobility" by the power and consequences of sin. Because of this, the writer of Hebrews wants us to be proactive. He wrote, "Therefore we also, since we are surrounded by so great a cloud of witnesses, let us lay aside every weight, and the sin which so easily ensnares us, and let us run with endurance the race that is set before us" (Hebrews 12:1).

If we are to run the race of the Christian life effectively, we must deal with sin before it immobilizes us. We need to lay aside the sin that hinders us from pleasing Him—starting today.

—*Bill Crowder*

Fact of Nature

In 1997 an Orca whale was reportedly spotted inducing tonic immobility in a great white shark, which subsequently drowned because of its immobility in the water.

✦ COMPASS POINT

Before sin immobilizes us spiritually, we must seek God's forgiveness and put it behind us.

"Try Some Ducks"

Guidebook Reading: 2 Corinthians 11:21–30

In the world you will have tribulation; but be of good cheer, I have overcome the world. —John 16:33

A man had rented a cottage with a large, light, airy cellar. A beautiful river ran by the cottage, and wonderful shade trees surrounded it. For five years he enjoyed the many blessings of the place and gladly paid the modest rent the landlord required. He bathed in the brook, fished in the pools, and rested in the shade. He was happy and contented. But then one day the river overflowed its banks, the cellar was flooded, and a dozen chickens he kept down there were all drowned. Suddenly he forgot all the past blessings and pleasures the place had afforded him, and all was gloom because of this temporary misfortune.

He bounced off to the landlord. "I've come," he said, "to notify you that I'm moving out."

Surprised, the landlord asked, "But why? I thought you appreciated everything so much these past five years."

"Yes," replied the tenant, "but it's different now; the river overflowed and all my hens are drowned."

The answer of the landlord completely disarmed the grumbler. He said, "Next time why don't you try ducks?"

Amusing? Yes, but what a lesson! Five years of enjoyment forgotten because of a few drowned hens. Have you been afflicted and suffered losses? Is everything blacked out by this passing misfortune? Have you forgotten the past benefits? Jesus said, "In the world you will have tribulation; but be of good cheer" (John 16:33). God knows what He is doing. This may be His way to make you appreciate past blessings. If your chickens drown, try some ducks!

—*M. R. DeHaan*

Fact *of* Nature

Many backyard farmers wonder whether to raise ducks or chickens. If that's a question you've wondered about, perhaps one of these books would help: *Storey's Guide to Raising Chickens* or *Storey's Guide to Raising Ducks.*

✳ COMPASS POINT

Disappointments in life can be expected—and they can teach us valuable lessons.

The Wonder of Nature

Guidebook Reading: Job 36:26–33

I have heard of You by the hearing of the ear, but now my eye sees You. —Job 42:5

Growing up around the woods and waters of the United States' Midwest, I've been fascinated with natural wildlife native to our region. But on a trip to the California coast, I found myself staring in breathtaking wonder at snorting elephant seals, barking sea lions, and a forest of silent redwoods. I watched pelicans soar in formation, and I saw migrating whales spouting in the distance. Together they are just a sampling of the millions of species that make up the intricate and delicate balance of nature.

According to the Bible, the variety of the natural world is designed to do far more than inspire childlike wonder. The mysteries of nature can help us come to terms with a God who allows inexpressible, unexplainable pain and suffering.

We see this in the epic story of Job. While he was suffering, Job didn't know that God had such a high regard for him that he allowed Satan to test his faith with a series of losses.

What emerges is this eventual, unavoidable conclusion: A Creator who has the wisdom and power to design the wonders of nature is great enough to be trusted with pain and suffering that are beyond our ability to understand. In awe, Job proclaimed, "I know that You can do everything" (42:2). We can trust that kind of God—no matter what.

—*Mart DeHaan*

Fact *of* Nature

Northern elephant seals were almost killed off in the 1800s through over-harvesting. From hundreds of thousands, they were down to under 100 in the 1890s. Mexico and the US teamed up to protect them, though, and now there are estimated to be 160,000 of them off the coast of California and Baja California.

✴ COMPASS POINT

Have you been challenged to trust God in spite of difficulties?

Lion of Judah

Guidebook Reading: Isaiah 31:1–5

Do not weep. Behold, the Lion of the tribe of Judah, the Root of David, has prevailed.
—REVELATION 5:5

The lounging lions in Kenya's Masai Mara game reserve looked harmless. They rolled on their backs in low-lying bushes. They rubbed their faces on branches as if trying to comb their magnificent manes. They drank leisurely from a stream. They strode slowly across dry, scrubby terrain as if they had all the time in the world. The only time I saw their teeth was when one of them yawned.

Fact *of* Nature

The Masai Mara National Reserve is a 583-square mile area in southwestern Kenya. It is home to zebras, wilde-beests, Thompson gazelles, elephants, lions, leopards, and rhinoceros.

Their serene appearance is deceiving, however. The reason they can be so relaxed is that they have nothing to fear—no shortage of food and no natural predators. The lions look lazy and listless, but they are the strongest and fiercest of all. One roar sends all other animals running for their lives.

Sometimes it seems as if God is lounging. When we don't see Him at work, we conclude that He's not doing anything. We hear people mock God and deny His existence, and we anxiously wonder why He doesn't defend himself. But God "will not be afraid of their voice nor be disturbed by their noise" (Isaiah 31:4). He has nothing to fear. One roar from Him, and His detractors will scatter like rodents.

If you wonder why God isn't anxious when you are, it's because He has everything under control. He knows that Jesus, the Lion of Judah, will triumph.

—*Julie Ackerman Link*

✷ COMPASS POINT

Nothing man can do will thwart God's purposes or plans.

Redwood Support

Guidebook Reading: Philippians 4:10–20

You have done well that you shared in my distress. —PHILIPPIANS 4:14

Sometimes the winds of trouble blow hard enough to topple us. Alone we might fall. But if we draw on the support of our brothers and sisters in Christ, we will have the strength we need to stand.

The late Ernie Harwell, longtime radio announcer for the Detroit Tigers baseball games and a strong believer in Jesus Christ, illustrated this in an article in the *Detroit Free Press* in the early 1990s when he wrote: "A Tigers rookie taught me something about reaching out during the past baseball season. The Tigers brought up Rich Rowland from their Toledo farm team. As I interviewed him, I found out that he was a lumberjack, or as he calls it, a tree-feller. He works in the redwood forest of California.

"He told me those giant redwood trees have shallow roots. 'How could they be so strong and have shallow roots?' I asked. 'Ernie,' he said, 'those trees are connected to each other by their roots. The roots of one tree reach out to the other trees, and they form a network of strength.' "

Christians need to uphold one another in times of stress. In Philippians 4:14, Paul expressed his gratitude for the way the believers in Philippi stood by him in his time of need. God used their support to encourage and strengthen the apostle.

Let's give one another redwood support!

—*Dave Egner*

Fact *of* Nature

The tallest redwoods need to exist in an area of dense and frequent fog. This provides moisture to the needles at the top, which are so far from the ground that the tree's system can't get enough water to them.

✳ COMPASS POINT

As believers in Jesus, we need to stick together for support.

Seeing God

Guidebook Reading: Psalm 19

The heavens declare the glory of God; and the firmament shows His handiwork.
—PSALM 19:1

One beautiful summer evening a small boy went fishing with his grandfather. The youngster was greatly impressed by the blue sky overhead, the fleecy white clouds drifting lazily along, and the shimmering surface of the lake rimmed by the greenery of the trees. As the sun began to set, the sight of that big orange ball of fire sinking in the western sky filled the boy's mind with many questions. (Most grandsons become quite inquisitive when they're with "Grandpa" in a setting like that.) After listening to some of his grandfather's answers, the boy was silent for a few moments. Then a puzzled expression came across his face. Looking up at the sky, he finally said, "Grandpa, can anyone see God?"

"Jimmy," he thoughtfully replied, "it's getting so I can't see anything but God!" He went on to explain what he meant, quoting Psalm 19:1: "The heavens declare the glory of God, and the firmament shows His handiwork."

All who are willing to open their eyes to the beauty, design, variety, order, complexity, and power in nature can see evidence of an all-wise, all-powerful Creator everywhere. And through the revelation He has given of himself in the Bible, they will learn that He is loving, merciful, gracious, and kind. Men and women of faith find Him not only everywhere but also in everything that comes their way. Knowing that all things work together for good to those who love the Lord, they can rejoice in any circumstance of life.

Happy is the person who can say with Grandpa, "It's getting so I can't see anything but God!"

—*Richard DeHaan*

Fact *of* Nature

While in orbit, a space shuttle travels at about 17,500 miles per hour, which allows the crew to see a sunrise or sunset every 45 minutes.

✳ COMPASS POINT

Looking for God? Look up and look around at His amazing creation.

The Devil's Soup Bowl

Guidebook Reading: Matthew 4:1–11

When [the devil] speaks a lie, he speaks from his own resources, for he is a liar and the father of it. —JOHN 8:44

While my sons-in-law and I were hiking in a state park one summer, we noticed a trail marker that pointed toward something called The Devil's Soup Bowl. Intrigued, we took off for this geologic formation. As we went, we joked about the kind of soup we might find in the bowl.

When we arrived, we discovered it to be a large sunken area of land—something like a deep lake without any water in it. We were rather disappointed to discover that The Devil's Soup Bowl was filled with nothing but trees and weeds.

The Devil's Soup Bowl is the perfect name for a formation that offers something of interest but ends up providing nothing, because the Devil is a deceiver. His menu is a bowl of tricks that delivers only empty promises and broken dreams.

Satan began his deceitful work of substituting nothing for something when he tricked Eve in the garden of Eden, and he has not changed his operating plan. He tried his deceit on Jesus, but the Lord resisted and "the devil left Him" (Matthew 4:9–11).

So how do you know if you are being offered one of Satan's lies? Test new ideas with Scripture. Consult with people you trust to be godly and wise. And pray. You don't want to taste what the Devil offers.

—*Dave Branon*

Fact *of* Nature

The Devil's Soup Bowl, which is located in the Yankee Springs Recreation Area in Western Michigan, is a formation left behind by glaciers. It is known as a "kettle" formation formed by a piece of glacier that broke off from the main glacier.

✳ COMPASS POINT

We've got to watch out for Satan's lies.

"Seasons" Greetings

Guidebook Reading: Ecclesiastes 3:1–8

To everything there is a season, a time for every purpose under heaven.
—ECCLESIASTES 3:1

I grew up on the West Coast of the United States. The possibility of snow for Christmas was so remote that my mom would point to fog in the early morning as evidence that the holidays were just around the corner.

My wife and I now live in the Midwest, where there's often a lot of snow when the yuletide season comes around. And I couldn't be happier with four distinct seasons. But not everyone shares my appreciation for the wonderful cycles of change God has built into nature for our good—especially when the bitter winds blow and the snow piles up outside.

In Ecclesiastes 3:1–8, Solomon acknowledged the cycles of life. He observed a time to sow and to reap, to weep and to laugh, to mourn and to dance, to gain and to lose, to keep silent and to speak, to love and to hate.

Just as God determines the weather, He also controls the cycles in our lives: "To everything there is a season, a time for every purpose under heaven" (Ecclesiastes 3:1). Do we resist those seasons and complain about the "snowy" conditions on the horizon? Or do we trust God and thank Him for whatever He has planned for us?

Whatever our situation is today, we can be thankful for God's seasons.

—*Dennis Fisher*

Fact *of* Nature

Where does the most snow fall in the US each year? The winner is Valdez, Alaska, which averages 327 inches a year. Others: Mt. Washington, New Hampshire (259 inches), Blue Canyon, California (240), Yakutat, Alaska (192), and Marquette, Michigan (143.3).

✳ COMPASS POINT

Seasons of weather and seasons of life are all God-directed times in which to serve Him.

Michael Cardinal

Guidebook Reading: Matthew 6:25–34

Look at the birds of the air . . . your heavenly Father feeds them. —Matthew 6:26

Twig by twig a cardinal constructed a bowl-shaped home in the bush outside my office window. Soon she laid an egg and kept it warm until it hatched. I named the little bird Michael. Although he was tiny, he had a huge appetite. His parents worked hard to keep him fed and safe. In a little less than two weeks, Michael was ready to leave, and I was there to witness the amazing event.

When Michael left, so did his mom and dad. The nest remained empty until the next spring. When Mama Cardinal returned, I was happy to see her but also sad. We had sold our house, and I was concerned that the new owners might chop down the bush. But my concern soon turned to amazement. As I dismantled my office, Mama Cardinal dismantled her nest. By the time we left, so had the cardinal family. Mama Cardinal's God-given instincts had told her to move.

Fact *of* Nature

The cardinal is such a popular bird that seven states have labeled it their state bird: Illinois, Indiana, Kentucky, North Carolina, Ohio, Virginia, and West Virginia.

This brought to mind another nature lesson. Using birds and lilies as examples, Jesus urged people not to worry. Since God takes care of birds, surely He will take care of His people (Matthew 6:26–30).

When concern for our own well-being leads to anxious thoughts, we can look at the birds and be assured of our value to God and of His care for us.

—*Julie Ackerman Link*

 COMPASS POINT

God's care for his wildlife creations can remind us how much He cares for us.

Johnny Appleseed

Guidebook Reading: Ecclesiastes 11:1–6

In the morning sow your seed, and in the evening do not withhold our hand; for you do not know which will prosper. —ECCLESIASTES 11:6

A kind and generous man named John Chapman carried on a project from 1801 to 1834 that is still bearing fruit today. His activities were so unusual that he has become a legendary figure. He appeared one April morning in Licking Spring, Ohio, having come from Massachusetts. Instead of claiming a piece of land for himself, he staked out a clearing, took some seeds out of a burlap bag he always carried, and began to plant them. After building a fence around the plot, he departed from Licking Spring as quietly as he had come. Chapman traveled through other towns and hamlets in Ohio, Indiana, and Michigan, and he followed the same simple procedure. From that time on, he became known as "Johnny Appleseed."

When John Chapman lived in Massachusetts, he had heard that only a few fruit trees existed in the Midwest, so he set out to remedy the situation. His untiring efforts in planting provided food for many people and brought beauty to barren locations.

An unknown author has written, "What the world needs are Christians who will be 'spiritual Johnny Appleseeds,' because men and women all around us are dying in sin. The Word of God is the seed that will give them life—food for their souls, gain for eternity, and beauty for ashes."

Fact *of* Nature

Johnny Appleseed obtained his apple seeds by visiting cider mills and taking the seeds from the pomace left over from the cider-making process.

May we be faithful in spreading the gospel along life's way by giving our testimony or by handing out gospel literature. Remember Johnny Appleseed. Let's be just as industrious, warmhearted, and selfless as we sow the seed of the Word—the most important seed of all.

—*Henry Bosch*

 COMPASS POINT

Taking seeds of the gospel to others is difficult but valuable work.

The Warbler's Witness

Guidebook Reading: Romans 1:18–25

O LORD, how manifold are Your works! In wisdom You have made them all. The earth is full of your possessions. —PSALM 104:24

A tiny bird, the lesser whitethroat warbler, summers in Germany and winters in Africa. As the days grow short, the adult birds head south, leaving their little ones behind. Several weeks later, the young fly across thousands of miles of unfamiliar land and sea to join their parents. How do they find a place totally unknown to them? Experiments have shown that they have an instinctive knowledge of longitude, latitude, and an ability to tell direction by the stars. God has given them a calendar, a clock, and all the navigational data they need to fly those thousands of uncharted miles to return to their parents' side.

The evolutionist says that our amazing and complex world—including the instinctive migrating characteristic of birds—developed by chance. But is this easier to accept than to believe that God created this amazing warbler and thousands of other such creatures? Isn't there a certain absurdity to ascribing this to chance?

God's wisdom is plainly observable in the works of His creation. His handiwork in nature speaks so strongly for His existence and power that Paul used it as an argument to establish man's guilt and condemnation. Paul wrote that man is without excuse if he does not respond in faith to the God who created all (Romans 1:20).

Our creator God deserves our recognition and our praise!

—Dave Egner

Fact of Nature

The whitethroat warbler averages 3,417 miles of traveling a year in order to get to Africa and back. By contrast, American travelers average a flying mileage of 2,000 miles a year.

✳ COMPASS POINT

There is no excuse not to praise God.

Where's the Power?

Guidebook Reading: Galatians 5:16–26

Are you so foolish? Having begun in the Spirit, are you now being made perfect by the flesh? —GALATIANS 3:3

Farmer Johnson smiled as he proudly strolled out of the hardware store with a brand-new chainsaw that was guaranteed to cut five big oak trees an hour. Twenty-four hours later, however, his smile was gone. With obvious frustration, Johnson was back at the store complaining that the saw would never cut five trees an hour. "Why, it only cut five trees all day long!" he said.

Somewhat puzzled, the storeowner stepped outside with the saw, gave the cord a rip, and fired up the steel-toothed beast. The deafening roar of the saw startled Johnson so badly that he stumbled trying to get away. "What's that noise?" he gasped.

Johnson's mistake in cutting down trees without starting up the chainsaw is similar to our foolishness when we try to follow Christ in our own strength. We get frustrated and spiritually exhausted when we try to make life work on our terms and by our schedule.

The Spirit of Christ who lives within all believers (Romans 8:9–11) can be very silent while we are trying to live by our own strength. Yet His presence can become real and powerful when we begin to trust Him for the life we cannot live.

Lord, we are so quick to forget the obvious. Renew us today in your strength and in your ways.

—*Mart DeHaan*

Fact of Nature

When was the first chainsaw invented? One news report suggests there was one as early as 1905. A few years later, a March 1918 edition of *Scientific American* magazine depicted a chainsaw on its cover.

✳ COMPASS POINT

Relying on our own strength—especially when compared to God's strength—doesn't make sense.

Call of the Chickadee

Guidebook Reading: 1 Thessalonians 5:12–24

Do not quench the Spirit. —1 Thessalonians 5:19

The black-capped chickadee has a surprising level of complexity in the noises it makes for alarm calls. Researchers found that chickadees use a high-frequency call to warn of danger in the air. Depending on the situation, the chickadee call can cue other birds about food that is nearby or predators that are perched too close for comfort.

Studies have also found that chickadees don't sense danger from large predators such as the great horned owl, because they are not likely to prey on such a petite bird. But smaller owls, which are closer to the size of the chickadee and more of a threat, prompt sentinel chickadees to repeat the alarm sound of their calls—the chickadee's distinctive "dee" note.

A similar level of awareness might serve us well. In the apostle Paul's first letter to the Thessalonians, he didn't just condemn the evils of the world. He also focused his attention on the matters of the heart that can do harm to us with barely a notice. "See that no one renders evil for evil to anyone, but always pursue what is good . . . Do not quench the Spirit . . . Test all things" (1 Thessalonians 5:15, 19, 21).

With the Spirit's help, let's keep attuned to every caution in the Word about our heart.

—*Mart DeHaan*

Fact *of* Nature

When a chickadee sees a fast-moving predator approaching, it sends out a high-pitched "dee." When other chickadees hear this, they freeze in position. They don't move until they hear another sound that means "all clear."

✳ COMPASS POINT

If we listen to the Spirit and obey the Word, we can avoid many troubles in life.

No God?

Guidebook Reading: Romans 1:14–20

What may be known of God is manifest in them, for God has shown it to them.
—ROMANS 1:19

Many years ago a friend sent me an article that included these words: "Some men say, 'There is no God.' All the wonders around you are accidental. No Almighty hand made a thousand billion stars. They made themselves. The surface of our land just happened to have topsoil, without which we would have no vegetables to eat, and no grass for the animals whose meat is our food.

"The inexhaustible envelope of air, only fifty miles deep and of exactly the right density to support human life, is just another law of physics. We have day and night because the earth spins at a given speed without slowing down. Who made this arrangement? Who tilts it so that we get seasons? The sun's fire does not generate too much heat so that we fry, but just enough so that we do not freeze. Who keeps its fire constant?

"The human heart will beat for seventy or eighty years without faltering. How does it get sufficient rest between beats? Who gave the human tongue flexibility to form words, and who made a brain to understand them? Is it all accidental? 'There is no God'? That's what some people say."

The Bible says, "In the beginning God created the heavens and the earth" (Genesis 1:1). The fool says, "There is no God" (Psalm 14:1).

—*Richard DeHaan*

Fact of Nature

A concept called "cosmological constant" suggests that the universe is such a finely tuned structure that tiny variations from what actually occurs in the universe would disallow life as we know it. This leads many to conclude that a supernatural model is more reasonable than a naturalistic, random-chance model.

✳ COMPASS POINT

Consider how difficult it is to believe that this intricate universe with all of its interlinked factors "just happened."

A Walk with Whitaker

Guidebook Reading: Genesis 1:20–25

Let birds fly above the earth across the face of the firmament of the heavens.
—GENESIS 1:20

When my dog Whitaker and I take our morning walk through the deep woods, the air is filled with sound. Birds of many species break the early morning silence with their songs.

Sometimes it's a steady chirp-chirp-chirp—probably a sparrow. It could be the lilting melody of a robin or the happy whistle of a proud cardinal. At times it's a sustained, single-note call from some unfamiliar bird. Then come the harsh squawks of a blue jay or the raucous caw of a raven. Then a little group of chickadees will flit their way through the trees, repeating their "chick-a-dee-dee-dee" sounds.

"Isn't God great?" I say to Whit, who seems to have chipmunks on his mind. I thank God for the great gift of hearing and the wonderful variety of sounds with which He fills His woods. He created thousands of varieties of birds, each with its own color and habits and call (Genesis 1:20–21). "God saw that it was good. And God blessed them" (vv. 21–22).

As I continue my walk with Whitaker, my heart is filled with thankfulness to God for the multitude of sights and sounds and colors and species that enrich our world. I praise Him for His creativity in not only forming our world but also in making it so beautiful—and good.

—*Dave Egner*

> ## Fact of Nature
>
> Of the 10,000 species of birds that have been discovered on earth, it has been estimated that about 925 of them have been observed in the US and Canada.

✵ COMPASS POINT

The beauty of the natural world, including the sights and sounds of birds, bring glory to God the creator.

Weed Control

Guidebook Reading: Mark 4:13–20

The cares of this world, the deceitfulness of riches, and the desires for other things entering in choke the word. —MARK 4:19

The parrotfeather is an attractive aquatic plant that looks like a forest of small fir trees growing on top of the water. In the springtime it produces a blanket of small, white flowers. But it's a noxious weed. It forms a dense mat of vegetation that covers the surface of lakes and ponds, crowding out native plants and destroying fish and wildlife habitat.

I recall hiking by a small lake in Washington State that was choked with parrotfeather plants. It occurred to me that, like that weed, "the cares of this world, the deceitfulness of riches, and the desires for other things entering in choke the word, and it becomes unfruitful," as Jesus taught in Mark 4:13–20.

Jesus was talking about how unbelievers receive the gospel, but His words can apply to us as well. Sometimes when we read God's Word, our minds are taken up with troubles, worries, and fears. The pressure of things to be done today and concerns about tomorrow's decisions are "weeds" that can choke the Word and make it unprofitable.

To control the weeds, we must ask God to quiet our hearts so we can pay attention to Him (Psalm 46:10). When we turn our worries over to God, we'll be free to enjoy His presence and hear what He has to say.

—*David Roper*

Fact *of* Nature

The parrotfeather, which is native to South America, is aggressively battled by some states and local governments in the US because it prevents some sport fish from migrating naturally and because it limits recreational use of the water. Some states have bans on the purchase of parrotfeather from plant dealers.

✳ COMPASS POINT

It takes clear thinking and a mind of reason to read and comprehend God's Word.

Lost in the Fog

Guidebook Reading: Proverbs 3:1–6

Trust in the Lord with all your heart, and lean not on your own understanding.
—PROVERBS 3:5

The fog was as thick as pea soup. Visibility was limited to a few feet, and the lake was as smooth as glass. The only sound to break the silence was the laughing of a loon across the lake.

I rowed for an hour around the shore, trying to catch fish in different areas, but the fish weren't biting. So I decided to go back to my cabin for a cup of coffee. I was at the mouth of a small inlet, which I knew was directly across the lake from the cottage. So I set out across the lake on a straight course (I thought) toward the dock.

After an hour of rowing, I was surprised when I arrived back at the mouth of the little stream from which I started. I had been going in a circle in the fog! I was so sure I knew where I was going, but after an hour I had gotten nowhere. If only I had taken my compass, instead of relying on my own sense of direction.

Proverbs 3:5 comes to mind: "Lean not on your own understanding." Without the Lord as your guide through the fog of life and without His Word as your compass, you will wander aimlessly.

So be sure to make Proverbs 3:6 your lifelong motto: "In all your ways acknowledge Him, and He shall direct your paths."

—*M. R. DeHaan*

Fact *of* Nature

One of the foggiest areas in the world is off the southeast coast of Newfoundland. The Grand Banks area is situated where the chilly Labrador Current clashes with the warm Gulf Stream to create sometimes impenetrable fog.

✳ COMPASS POINT

Looking for direction? Trust the One who knows the way.

By Dawn's Early Light

Guidebook Reading: Psalm 148

Glorify the Lord in the dawning light. — ISAIAH 24:15

Dressed for warmth and walking the path by memory, I crept through the pre-dawn darkness to sit at a quiet place in Michigan's north woods. I settled at the base of a sixty-foot white pine, got comfortable, and joined the silent forest. As day began to break, discernible shapes emerged from the darkness. Inch by inch the dawn appeared, and with it came the awakening of the forest.

Here and there birds began to sing. A flock of majestic geese flew low to the horizon, punctuating the sky with their busy conversation. A doe and her fawns moved soundlessly along the pine break. A red squirrel stared at me and flicked his tail.

How could I experience the majestic panorama of God's creation and not praise Him? Quietly I did so, and my mind was shouting glory to His name for all the angels to hear. Yet compared with the giant beech trees, lacy cedars, whip-thin poplars, and leafy ferns, my praise seemed insignificant. What could my words add to the wonder of the perky chickadee and the fleet-footed rabbit?

The author of Psalm 148 understood that all nature reflects the Creator's power and greatness. On that cool fall day I was privileged to join creation in glorifying God by dawn's early light.

—*Dave Egner*

Fact *of* Nature

At sunrise the light of the sun passes through the largest amount of the earth's atmosphere. As this happens, the reds and the oranges of the light spectrum scatter more easily, thus producing brilliant light shows.

✳ COMPASS POINT

Think about it. Our praise can never be as majestic as the praise that comes from God's natural world.

A Common Enemy

Guidebook Reading: Ephesians 4:17–32

Do not let the sun go down on your wrath, nor give place to the devil.
—EPHESIANS 4:27

The early morning racket was so loud that I rolled out of bed and went to the front door to see what was happening. I knew about their longstanding argument, but I had never heard them go at it like this before.

There in the trees in front of our house it appeared that the crows and the blue jays were quarreling again. Their war of words and wings had escalated beyond anything I had seen before. I watched the "reserves" fly in and take positions in the branches. The actual bombing and strafing was concentrated in the upper regions of a big oak. But then I saw something I hadn't expected. A pair of huge brown wings made a tactical retreat to a nearby branch. That was no crow, and this was not the usual spat between the crows and jays. They weren't fighting each other on this Sunday morning. They had found a common enemy. They had located an owl, and their mutual dislike for one another was lost in a conflict of greater proportions. Together the crows and the blue jays had combined forces against the owl.

That scene impressed me as being one of nature's striking parallels to a spiritual reality. As believers in Christ, we have a common enemy, and he is reason enough to make us forget our differences. That's implied in the fourth chapter of Ephesians, where Paul urges us to put away our personal dislikes, our anger, and our self-centered interests. When we yield to these fleshly impulses, we "give place to the devil" (v. 27). And the Devil likes nothing more than to have us fighting one another rather than him.

—*Mart DeHaan*

> ## Fact *of* Nature
>
> Blue jays and owls don't get along. Sometimes blue jays will gang up on an owl and bother it until it flies out of their territory. Some days it feels like blue jays do this to humans too!

✳ COMPASS POINT
Fight Satan, not fellow believers.

Light of Creation

Guidebook Reading: Job 37:1–18

[God] does great things, and unsearchable, marvelous things without number.
—JOB 5:9

Among the wonders of Jamaica is a body of water called Luminous Lagoon. By day it is a nondescript bay on the country's northern coast. By night it is a marvel of nature.

If you visit there after dark, you notice that the water is filled with millions of phosphorescent organisms. Whenever there is movement, the water and the creatures in the bay glow. When fish swim past your boat, for example, they light up like waterborne fireflies. As the boat glides through the water, the wake shines brightly.

The wonder of God's creation leaves us speechless, and this is just a small part of the total mystery package of God's awesome handiwork as spelled out in Job 37 and 38. Listen to the Lord explain His role in nature's majesty: "Do you know how God controls the clouds and makes His lightning flash?" (37:15 NIV); "What is the way to the abode of light? And where does darkness reside?" (38:19 NIV).

God's majestic creations—whether dazzling lightning or glowing fish—are mysteries to us. But as God reminded Job, all of the wonders of our world are His creative handiwork.

When we observe God's amazing creation, our only response can be that of Job: These are "things too wonderful for me" (42:3).

—*Dave Branon*

Fact *of* Nature

The Luminous Lagoon (also known as Glistening Waters) is one of at least three bioluminescent bays in the Caribbean. Two others are in Puerto Rico.

✸ COMPASS POINT

The mysterious and fantastic elements of creation cause us to stand in awe of God.

A Sad Split

Guidebook Reading: Malachi 2:10–16

Let none deal treacherously with the wife of his youth. —MALACHI 2:15

The drama played out in a nest of bald eagles monitored by a webcam. A beloved eagle family, viewed by many via the Internet, was breaking up. After raising several offspring in previous seasons, the parents again laid new eggs in the spring. But then a young female invaded their happy home. When Dad started cavorting with her, Mom disappeared and the life in the abandoned eggs died.

In an Internet chat room, questions and accusations flew wildly. Everyone who loved the pair was distraught. Biologists warned the amateur eagle enthusiasts not to attribute human values to birds. But everyone did. We all wanted the original couple to reunite. Everyone seemed to "know" that the family unit is sacred.

As chat room members expressed their sadness, I wondered if they knew that God feels much the same way about human family breakups. I also wondered about myself: Why did I feel more sadness over the eagles than over the fractured human families in my community? Clearly, I need to revise my priorities.

In Malachi 2 we see God's view of marriage. It symbolizes His covenant with His people (v. 11). He takes it very seriously—and so should we.

—*Julie Ackerman Link*

Fact *of* Nature

Bald eagle pairs remain together until one dies, so it was very unusual for this male eagle to abandon one female for another. Wild bald eagles may live as long as 30 years.

✳ COMPASS POINT

Can we reexamine our view of marriage and be reminded of how sacred it is before God?

Register Rock

Guidebook Reading: Hebrews 11:32–40

We are surrounded by so great a cloud of witnesses. —HEBREWS 12:1

Along the old Oregon Trail in Idaho there is a marker—a giant lava boulder known locally as Register Rock. It's located in an area that was one of the favorite overnight camping areas for westbound immigrants who traveled the trail in the nineteenth century. Travelers often inscribed their names on the rock as a memorial to their passage. Register Rock stands as a monument to their courage and tenacity.

When I think of Register Rock, I think of other pilgrims who have passed by us on their journey. Hebrews 11 lists some of those hardy souls—Gideon, Barak, Samson, Jephthah, David, and Samuel, to name a few.

But there are other, more recent pilgrims: my mother and father, my fifth-grade Sunday school teacher Mrs. Lincoln, my youth leader John Richards, my mentors Ray Stedman and Howard Hendricks, and a host of others I could name. They may not have inscribed their names on rocks, but they are written in my memory.

The author of Hebrews reminds us to remember "pilgrims" who have gone before us, especially those "who have spoken the word of God" to us, and to consider "the outcome of their conduct" (Hebrews 13:7). And, most important, the writer encourages us to follow their faith.

—*David Roper*

Fact of Nature

Today, Register Rock is fenced off to protect it from modern-day visitors who might want to add their names to those of the explorers of the 1800s. The best view of it is in an 1891 painting by Frederic Remington, which shows the rock in its natural state.

✵ COMPASS POINT

Say thanks for the people who have left their marks on your life.

Giants of the Deep

Guidebook Reading: Job 41:1–11

God created great sea creatures and every living thing that moves. —Genesis 1:21

The blue whale is the largest animal that has ever lived. Some are 100 feet long and can weigh over 175 tons. The biggest one ever measured had a heart the size of a Volkswagen Beetle!

In Genesis we are told, "God created great sea creatures and every living thing that moves, with which the waters abounded, according to their kind" (1:21).

When the Creator revealed himself to Job in his time of suffering, He used the giants of the deep, including the mysterious Leviathan, to illustrate His divine power, His unsearchable nature, and His incomparable character. "Shall one not be overwhelmed at the sight of [Leviathan]? No one is so fierce that he would dare stir him up. Who then is able to stand against Me? . . . Everything under heaven is Mine" (Job 41:9–11).

God uses the whale, the Leviathan, and all the giants of the deep to remind us of how awesome He is as Creator of the universe (Romans 1:20). The One who made creatures that cannot be controlled is himself beyond our control and understanding.

Just as a frightening thunderstorm makes us stand in awe of the Creator, so should the blue whale. All of God's creation points to His eternal power.

—*Dennis Fisher*

Fact *of* Nature

The blue whale population in the world today is about 15,000. At one time there were approximately 350,000 of those huge mammals swimming the oceans. The blue whale is considered an endangered species.

 COMPASS POINT

Looking for a good reason to believe in God? Visit a zoo.

Show Your Colors

Guidebook Reading: 2 Corinthians 4:7–18

It is no longer I who live, but Christ lives in me. —GALATIANS 2:20

The Bible teaches that God lives in the believer so that Christ may be revealed in him. As the dark passions of the old nature are crucified, the full glories of His presence become increasingly evident.

With the changing of the seasons, nature's "signs of the times" present an interesting parallel to this truth. Although I do not enjoy raking up what falls in the fall, I always anticipate seeing the splendor and beauty that marks the last few months of the year. Trees that have been green since May gradually change expression, then seemingly burst into autumn emotions. One by one they form a prismatic procession of reds, oranges, yellows, and golds.

Casually observing the ordinary maple, someone might exclaim, "I didn't know you had it in you!" Botanists tell us, however, that these brilliant colors have been there all along. Masked by the denser greens, they can't express themselves until the chlorophyll deteriorates. Once this begins, the more stable pigments in the leaf become apparent.

In much the same way, the child of God can manifest the red and gold hues of virtue that were so evident in the Savior's life from the cross to the crown. They are revealed as we mortify the deeds of the flesh daily and yield ourselves to the Lord. To display the brilliant qualities of a Christlike character, we must cease to live solely by our own intellect, emotions, and will.

Maybe thinking about autumn colors will help those who are indwelt by God's Spirit to show ours.

—*Mart DeHaan*

> ### Fact *of* Nature
>
> At the same time that the chlorophyll process stops in leaves, eliminating the green pigment, additional chemical changes can occur. New pigments can also be added—brighter reds, purples, and oranges—to complement the colors that show up when the green is gone.

✳ COMPASS POINT

Are we showing the brightness of Christ in our lives, or are we masking His presence with our sin?

The Rock and the Flourishing Palms

Guidebook Reading: Psalm 62:1–8

The Lord is my rock and my fortress and my deliverer. —2 Samuel 22:2, 3

In the Kofa Mountains of Arizona, jutting majestically from the red granite sides of a 2500-foot canyon, are the only native palms in the entire state. For years it has been a mystery how those tropical plants can flourish and remain so strong and luxuriant on the dark, almost perpendicular sides of this narrow gorge. The fact that the sun reaches them only two hours a day makes their hearty growth even more of a puzzle. Botanists finally concluded that the stone walls must reflect enough light and store enough warmth throughout the day to enable these trees to thrive in the cold shadows of the canyon.

In these palms we may see a parable. Believers who live in close fellowship with God can stand the oppressive darkness of adverse circumstances. Why? Because the Rock on which they are founded retains all the warmth of heavenly love and comfort they need to keep them in spiritual health. Profitable lives of Christian testimony develop in verdant beauty even in places of great privation. Finding their sufficiency in the Savior, believers produce the luxuriant leaves of witness and the excellent fruit of praise. Yes, in the restricted crevices of pain where the sun of prosperity seldom shines, we often discover the loveliest "trees of righteousness" (Isaiah 61:3).

Founded on God—the Rock of their strength and salvation—redeemed souls can remain joyful and productive even in the darkest circumstances. They are indeed a wonder to the world as they continue to flourish like the Kofa palms.

—*Henry Bosch*

Fact of Nature

It's difficult to find out the age of the Kofa palms because that kind of tree does not produce growth rings. When the trees were last counted, there were 42 of them, some with a circumference of 20 feet.

✸ COMPASS POINT

In the midst of life's darkness—even then—we can shine God's light.

Springboard of Praise

Guidebook Reading: Genesis 2:1–15

The LORD God took the man and put him in the garden of Eden to tend and keep it. —GENESIS 2:15

In his historical novel *Chesapeake*, James Michener tells the story of multiple generations living near a marsh. One character, Chris Pflaum, is introduced as a restless thirteen-year-old sitting in class waiting for summer break. But when the teacher reads a poem by Sidney Lanier, the boy's heart is stirred.

> *As the marsh-hen secretly builds on the watery sod,*
> *Behold I will build me a nest on the greatness of God:*
> *I will fly in the greatness of God as the marsh-hen flies*
> *In the freedom that fills all the space 'twixt the marsh and*
> *the skies.*

When Chris grew up, this poem motivated him to work tirelessly to preserve the precious wetlands and the wildlife he loved.

Lanier's words stir the heart because they use nature as a springboard of praise to the Creator. But, unfortunately, our living planet can be neglected and exploited. God's mandate to Adam has been passed on to all believers: "The LORD God . . . put him in the garden of Eden to tend and keep it" (Genesis 2:15). The words tend and keep mean "to cultivate as servants."

We are to care for and guard God's creation as responsible stewards.

—*Dennis Fisher*

Fact of Nature

In the US, both state and federal laws protect wetlands from being destroyed by development. They are protected not only because of the wildlife that live in wetlands but also because wetlands filter pollutants and protect surrounding lands from flooding.

 COMPASS POINT

Consider how you can become a better steward of the resources God has given us.

A Path Through the Woods

Guidebook Reading: Exodus 13:17–22

The Lord went before them . . . to lead the way. —EXODUS 13:21

Daddy built a tepee in the woods for five-year-old Bree and her three-year-old sister Abby. Then he constructed a playhouse for them in a nearby fallen tree. When the leaves were off the trees, the children could see the family cabin from their hideouts. But in the tangled underbrush of summer, the girls thought they were deep in the scary woods.

So Dad took an ax and clippers into the woods and cut a trail from the back door of the cabin to the playhouse, then to the tepee, and back to the cabin. The sisters felt safe and secure because the path was easy to follow.

We may wish that God would blaze a trail for us through the deep woods of the future, but that's not His way. He doesn't leave us without guidance, though. We learn something of His loving character when we see what He did for Israel as they left Egypt. He "went before them" and showed the way by the pillars of cloud and fire (Exodus 13:21).

Today we aren't led by dramatic signs like fire and cloud. But God has given something better— the indwelling presence of the Holy Spirit (John 14:26; Galatians 5:16, 18).

You may never see a clear path through life. But as you follow the Holy Spirit's leading and God's written Word, you'll know where to turn when the way isn't clear.

—Dave Egner

Fact *of* Nature

The tepee was used by nomadic Native Americans who lived in the Great Plains. It was constructed in a way that made it easily portable when the people moved to a new location. The word itself comes from the language of the Lakota, a part of the Sioux confederation of tribes.

✸ COMPASS POINT

Do you see God's guidance ahead? It's there. Pray and read the Guidebook.

Elephants Down

Guidebook Reading: Jonah 4

On the seventh day you shall rest, that your ox and your donkey may rest.
—EXODUS 23:12

When rainy-season storms caused flooding in a nature preserve in Thailand, seven elephant calves became unfortunate victims. As they tried to ford a river at their usual crossing point, dangerous currents swept them over a 250-foot waterfall. Wildlife advocates said the loss could have been prevented. A spokesperson for the Thailand Wildlife Fund complained that the protective barriers, which had been built at the crossing where four other young elephants had died earlier, were useless.

Fact *of* Nature

There are currently about 7,700 elephants living in Thailand, where the elephant is a symbol of the nation's past. A hundred years ago there were more than 300,000 elephants in the country.

Long before animal protection became a global issue, the story of Jonah shows the attention our Creator gives to all His creatures. As the story ends, the Lord expresses concern not only for the citizens of Nineveh but also for their livestock (Jonah 4:11). And earlier God gave Moses laws that extended certain protections even to animals (Exodus 23:4–5, 12).

Though humans alone are made in the image of God, the story of Jonah and other Bible texts show a link between caring for people and animals. The Creator gives us reason to provide appropriate, though different, attention to both.

The conclusion seems clear. If God cares even for livestock, how can we ignore the needs of any person for whom His Son died?

—*Mart DeHaan*

✳ COMPASS POINT

God made all the animals and He watches over them, but He has a special place in His heart for us.

Man-Made Hail

Guidebook Reading: Ephesians 4:17–29

Let all bitterness, wrath, anger, clamor, and evil speaking be put away from you, with all malice. —Ephesians 4:31

The hail produced by a violent thunderstorm can devastate crops, injure animals, pound people, damage aircraft, and dent cars. These ice balls come in all sizes, from a tiny pellet to the size of a grapefruit. Hailstones are formed when a cloud is blown by a violent updraft, causing it to rise into the freezing zone in the atmosphere. At that point, ice builds up around the nucleus of a snow pellet. The higher and longer the thunderstorm tosses the particles around, the larger and more destructive the hailstones become.

The hail of a thundercloud and a person's angry words have a lot in common. Under certain circumstances, violent winds of bitterness and hurt feelings can carry the level of anger higher and higher. Soon pent-up emotions spill out in verbal attacks on others, either directly or behind their backs.

Ephesians 4 speaks of the damage that anger can do. Repressing it and allowing it to seethe in our hearts gives the Devil an opportunity to work in our lives (v. 27). Bitterness, wrath, and anger grieve the Holy Spirit (vv. 30–31).

Verse 32 tells how to control this powerful emotion before it creates "man-made hail"—by "forgiving one another, even as God in Christ forgave you." Immediate forgiveness is the key to controlling anger.

Harboring bitter feelings and nurturing grudges only produces verbal storms that cause injury. So deal with your anger quickly—before it grows into a hailstorm of hurt.

—*Kurt DeHaan*

> ## Fact *of* Nature
>
> The largest hailstone discovered in the US was an 8-inch-thick ice ball that fell in 2010 in South Dakota. That hailstone weighed almost 2 pounds and was 18 inches in circumference.

✴ COMPASS POINT

Self-control and forgiveness can calm the angry heart.

God and the Ravens

Guidebook Reading: 1 Kings 17:1–6

And it will be that you shall drink from the brook, and I have commanded the ravens to feed you there. —1 KINGS 17:4

The Associated Press carried this story under the heading "Crow Feeds Dog":

For six days a puppy trapped in an animal snare was kept alive by a crow. Both animals belong to a couple living at a road construction camp. After the dog disappeared recently the pet crow stopped eating normally. It would take a bit of food in its beak, fly off, and return a short time later to fetch another scrap. One day they followed it and were led to the spot where the dog lay trapped.

Fact of Nature

In 2006 a crow named Tata, which was reported to be 59 years old, died. That figure cannot be verified, but researchers say it could be true. Tata never lived in the wild, but he lived with a family his entire life.

The article then concluded, "The earliest reference to this type of thing was the feeding of Elijah by the ravens."

The provision of bread and meat for the prophet Elijah was certainly a marvelous thing. Yet as children of the heavenly Father, we can know something even more wonderful—God's daily supply of all our needs.

The Lord said to Elijah, "I have commanded the ravens to feed you there" (1 Kings 17:4). And the apostle Paul, writing to believers at Philippi, declared, "God shall supply all your need" (4:19). God may not actually use birds for this purpose today, but He does have His "ravens," whereby His bountiful provisions are delivered to us.

The Lord expects us, however, to be diligent in fulfilling our responsibility as well. His Word therefore emphasizes, "Work with your own hands" (1 Thessalonians 4:11). Once we have done our part, we may rest in the assurance of the Lord's gracious supply, for He has His "ravens" in every age!

—*Richard DeHaan*

✸ COMPASS POINT

God's provisions for us should lead us to trust Him and praise Him.

Embroidery of Earth

Guidebook Reading: Isaiah 41:17–20

I will plant in the wilderness the cedar and the acacia tree, the myrtle and the oil tree. —ISAIAH 41:19

Near one of the most majestic sites in nature is a botanical garden of awe-inspiring beauty. On the Canadian side of Niagara Falls is the Floral Showhouse. Inside the greenhouse is a vast array of beautiful flowers and exotic plants. In addition to the flora my wife and I observed while visiting there, something else caught our attention—the wording of a plaque.

It reads: "Enter, friends, and view God's pleasant handiwork, the embroidery of earth." What a marvelous way to describe the way our Creator favored this globe with such jaw-dropping beauty!

The "embroidery of earth" includes such far-ranging God-touches as the verdant rainforests of Brazil, the frigid beauty of Arctic Circle glaciers, the flowing wheat fields of the North American plains, and the sweeping reaches of the fertile Serengeti in Africa. These areas, like those described in Isaiah 41, remind us to praise God for His creative handiwork.

Scripture also reminds us that the wonder of individual plants is part of God's work. From the rose (Isaiah 35:1) to the lily (Matthew 6:28) to the myrtle, cypress, and pine (Isaiah 41:19–20), God colors our world with a splendorous display of beauty. Enjoy the wonder. And spend some time praising God for the "embroidery of earth."

—*Dave Branon*

Fact *of* Nature

On average, 600,000 gallons of water go over the Horseshoe Falls at Niagara every second. In a little over 2 seconds, the water going over the falls equals the amount of water used in the city of Chicago in one day.

✳ COMPASS POINT

Spend some time praising God for the "embroidery of earth."

God's Signature

Guidebook Reading: Genesis 1:27–31

God saw everything that He had made, and indeed it was very good.
—GENESIS 1:31

Displayed on the wall of my friends' lake house is a collection of pictures. Each one of the photos is of a sunset, taken from their deck during various seasons. While each is strikingly beautiful, no two are identical. When I look at them, I am reminded of what another friend once called a sunset: "God's beautiful signature at the end of a day."

God writes His signature on each sunset and on each of His unique children as well. I never grow tired of discovering how every person I meet is so delightfully different. God is infinitely creative, and the variety in our personalities, senses of humor, abilities, and preferences in music and sports are all handcrafted by Him.

In the body of Christ we see how a diversity of spiritual gifts still have a common bond and can work together for God's purposes to bring Him glory. In 1 Corinthians 12:4–6, we read, "There are diversities of gifts, but the same Spirit. There are differences of ministries, but the same Lord. And there are diversities of activities, but it is the same God who works all in all."

God's signature that is so evident in nature is also present in His people. Let's celebrate the differences that make each of His children unique.

—*Cindy Hess Kasper*

Fact *of* Nature

According to researchers at the National Oceanic and Atmospheric Administration (NOAA), late fall and winter are the best times for optimum sunrises and sunsets over most of the US.

✱ COMPASS POINT

God's creative touch made each of us different from the other, which results in a multi-talented team of people to do His work.

Of Flies and Sparrows

Guidebook Reading: Matthew 10:24–31

Do not fear therefore; you are of more value than many sparrows.
—MATTHEW 10:31

Did you ever take a moment to consider God's special care in designing even His smallest creatures? When you see how adequately they are equipped, you will be encouraged to entrust your life completely to Him.

I once heard Bible teacher and physician Walter L. Wilson (1881–1969) describe the mechanism that enables a common housefly to walk upside down on the ceiling or keep its hold on the smooth glass of a window. He said that on a fly's six feet are approximately a thousand tiny hairs. Each hair is hollow and has a little sack containing a sticky substance located high up in the foot. As the fly lights on a very slick surface, the pressure forces out a tiny bit of "glue" through each of those tubular hairs. Thus it is able to hold tightly to anything, even when upside down. Wilson summed it up by saying that if the great God of the universe would devise such a simple though intricate scheme for a tiny insect's survival, surely He will more than adequately provide for all our needs.

Through the pine trees outside my study window, I often see sparrows flitting about. I am impressed by how small and insignificant they are! Yet according to Jesus' words in Matthew 10:31, not one of them falls to the ground without the heavenly Father noticing it. I can draw only one conclusion: If God in heaven is concerned about the little birds of the air, isn't it reasonable to believe that He will supply all the needs of His children?

So take courage. You are of much more value than lowly flies and little sparrows.

—*Paul Van Gorder*

Fact *of* Nature

The common housefly, or *Musca domestica*, lives about a month on average. It's hard to sneak up on a fly because it has compound eyes that allow it to have a viewing area of 360 degrees.

✸ COMPASS POINT

Is it possible to feel appreciated because of a lesson about flies?

Bombardier Beetle

Guidebook Reading: Job 12:7–13

In [God's] hand is the life of every living thing. —JOB 12:10

Have you ever stopped to consider the amazing features God placed in the animals He created? Job did, and one of the most interesting he wrote about is the ostrich. Despite its apparent lack of good sense and its eccentric parenting skills, its offspring survive (39:13–16). And despite its membership in the bird family, it can't fly—but it can outrun a horse (v. 18).

Another remarkable creature is the bombardier beetle. This African insect shoots two common materials, hydrogen peroxide and hydroquinone, from twin storage tanks in its back. Apart, these substances are harmless; together, they blind the beetle's predators. A special nozzle inside the beetle mixes the chemicals, enabling it to bombard its foe at amazing speeds! And the little guy can rotate his "cannon" to fire in any direction.

How can this be? How is it that a rather dull-witted ostrich survives despite a seeming inability to care for its young while the bombardier beetle needs a sophisticated chemical reaction to ensure its continued presence on earth? It's because God's creative abilities know no boundaries. "He commanded and they were created," the psalmist tells us (148:5). From the ostrich to the beetle, God's creative work is clear for all to see.

"Praise the name of the Lord" (148:13).

—*Dave Egner*

Fact of Nature

A debate rages between creationists and evolutionists regarding this insect. The bombardier beetle appears to prove that it had to have a designer, but evolutionists have prepared a complicated, speculative explanation to posit that it could have evolved.

✷ COMPASS POINT

Every new example of God's creative genius should cause us to praise Him anew.

"Dead Sea" Christian?

Guidebook Reading: John 7:37–46

He who believes in Me, as the Scripture has said, out of his heart will flow rivers of living water. —JOHN 7:38

The Dead Sea, also known as the Salt Sea, is unique among all bodies of water in the world. It contains hardly any organic life (other than some primitive microbes). It definitely does not need any "No Fishing" signs!

What accounts for this unusual condition? The answer lies in the fact that the Dead Sea has absolutely no outlets! Water pours into this area from rivers and streams, including the Jordan River in the north, the Arnon in the east, and the Kidron in the west. But nothing flows out! Many inlets plus no outlets equals a Dead Sea!

This formula from nature may also be applied to the child of God, and it explains why many believers are so unfruitful and lacking in spiritual vitality. People often wonder how it is possible for some folks to attend Bible conferences, listen to sound religious broadcasts, study the Scriptures, and continually take in the Word as it is preached from the pulpit, and yet seem so "lifeless" and unproductive in their Christian lives. Such individuals are like the Dead Sea: they have several "inlets" but no "outlets"! To be vibrant and useful believers, we must not only "take in" all we can, we must also "give out" in service to others!

May the Lord make you a refreshing fountain from which thirsty souls may drink. Indwelt by the Holy Spirit, you possess the "water of life" and can be a channel of blessing to those in need. From your heart of love, pour out to others that which you have first received from God. If you do, you'll never become a "Dead Sea" Christian.

—*Richard DeHaan*

Fact *of* Nature

The Dead Sea has a salt content of about 33 percent, making it the third saltiest lake on earth. Lake Assal in Djibouti (southern tip of the Red Sea) and Garabagazkol (a bay of the Caspian Sea) are saltier.

✸ COMPASS POINT

From a heart of love, pour out to others that which you have first received from God.

Little Sponges

Guidebook Reading: Deuteronomy 11:13–23

You shall teach [these words of mine] to your children . . . when you walk by the way, when you lie down, and when you rise up. —DEUTERONOMY 11:19

Most household sponges we use today are synthetic; therefore, many people are surprised to learn that real sponges were at one time living sea animals. When a live sponge is removed from the sea and its living matter is cleaned out, it becomes useful for household purposes. The skeleton that remains, with its open-celled structure, can soak up and absorb liquid.

Children are like sponges. They soak up attitudes and ideas with which they come in contact. We must be careful, therefore, about what is allowed to fill their minds.

What are your children or grandchildren absorbing in your home? What are they getting from the many forms of media available to them? Also, as they listen to your conversations, what kind of words and attitudes are being taken in? Are you setting a good example of love for the Lord and concern for others? Is there a warm spiritual emphasis in your home? Are you doing what you can to fill their hearts with God's Word?

When children become adults, they will give out what they have taken in during their formative and impressionable years. Let's make sure those little "sponges" in our homes soak up what is pure, wholesome, and uplifting.

—*Richard DeHaan*

Fact *of* Nature

Sponges grow on the ocean floor. When the creatures are harvested, sponge divers leave the part of the sponge that is anchored to the ocean floor intact so that the sponge will regenerate and grow back to its original form.

✳ COMPASS POINT

It's important to have a strong spiritual effect on the children in your life.

Be Careful!

Guidebook Reading: 1 Corinthians 10:1–13

Let him who thinks he stands take heed lest he fall. —1 Corinthians 10:12

Several years ago my wife Carolyn and I were hiking on Mount Rainier in Washington when we came to a swollen glacial stream. Someone had flattened one side of a log and dropped it across the stream to form a crude bridge, but there was no handrail and the log was slippery.

The prospect of walking on the wet log was frightening, and Carolyn didn't want to cross. But she found the courage, and slowly, carefully she inched her way to the other side.

On the way back we had to walk on the same log, and she did so with the same care. "Are you afraid?" I asked.

"Of course," she replied, "that's what keeps me safe." Again, fully aware of the danger, she made her way to safety.

Much of life poses moral danger for us. We should never assume in any situation that we're incapable of falling. "Let him who thinks he stands take heed lest he fall" (1 Corinthians 10:12). Given the opportunity and circumstances, any of us are capable of falling into any sin. To believe otherwise is sheer folly.

We must watch and pray and arm ourselves for every occasion by putting our total trust in God (Ephesians 6:13). "God is faithful" (1 Corinthians 10:13), and He will give us the strength to keep from falling.

—*David Roper*

Fact *of* Nature

Mount Rainier, the highest mountain in the Lower 48 states, has an elevation of 14,411 feet (21st highest in the world). It is a volcanic mountain that last erupted in 1894.

✳ COMPASS POINT

Recognizing the danger of sin is a first step toward avoiding it.

Creation: NT Style

Guidebook Reading: Ephesians 1:3–6

He chose us in Him before the foundation of the world. —EPHESIANS 1:4

When we think about the marvel of creation—how God spoke the universe into existence and formed the earth and everything in it—we think most often of Old Testament accounts. But it is encouraging to examine the New Testament to see how that part of the Bible refers to creation. Here is a look at some key passages:

"I will utter things kept secret from the foundation of the world" (Matthew 13:35). God reveals things to us that He had kept secret since before creation.

"Come, you blessed of My Father, inherit the kingdom prepared for you from the foundation of the world" (Matthew 25:34). Before the earth was created, God knew each of us—and He knew our future.

"He chose us in Him before the foundation of the world" (Ephesians 1:4). Before the work of creation even began, God was aware of each of His eventual children.

These New Testament verses comfort us with the truth that God's knowledge of us and His eternal mysteries about us point toward His special creation of mankind as described in Genesis. We can do nothing but bow in awe before One whose knowledge and creative ability are eternal in nature and boundless in power.

Creation: New Testament style—still another reason to give God praise!

—*Dave Branon*

Fact *of* Nature

Mark 10:6, "But from the beginning of the creation, God made them male and female," is another New Testament reference to God's creation of mankind during the creation event.

✳ COMPASS POINT

Created in God's image, mankind is the crown of creation.

Of Ants and Elephant Seals

Guidebook Reading: Proverbs 6:6–11

Awake to righteousness, and do not sin, for some do not have the knowledge of God.
—1 CORINTHIANS 15:34

According to recent research, elephant seals spend almost all of their lives sleeping. *Science News* magazine reports, "Male elephant seals measure 16 feet from trunk-like nose to flipper, and they weigh about 3 tons. Occasionally, a seal will use a front flipper—incredibly tiny for such a massive creature—to scratch itself or flip sun-shielding sand on its body." Otherwise these huge animals are basically motionless. The article goes on to state that because they don't eat while on land during the breeding season, they sleep most of the time. Besides scratching, dirt-flipping, rolling over, or taking an infrequent short stroll, these ponderous animals seldom move.

By contrast, the little ant seems tireless as it goes about its industrious work of storing up food for the colony. The writer of Proverbs commends the diligence of the ant, citing her active ways as a model for people who would live wisely and want to make their lives count.

There's a spiritual lesson in all of this. Those who pattern their service after the ant are productive and get things done for the Lord. But there are others, like the elephant seal, who scarcely move. Regarding service, they seem to be barely alive spiritually, as if they are conserving their energy for some gigantic effort later on. But the time to get busy for Christ is always now, even though our talents may be small and our opportunities few.

Let's model our lives after the ant, not the elephant seal.

—*Dave Egner*

Fact of Nature

Imagine if an elephant seal could do what the ant does: Lift 20 times its own weight. For a male elephant seal, that would be 60 tons— about the weight of a 156-foot yacht.

✳ COMPASS POINT

There is so much to do for the Lord, and it's up to us to do it.

You Can Count on It!

Guidebook Reading: 1 Kings 8:54–61

Blessed be the Lord . . . There has not failed one word of all His good promise.
—1 KINGS 8:56

A man who lived in northern Michigan went for a walk in a densely forested area. When darkness began to settle in, he decided it was time to head for home. He was familiar with hiking in the woods and felt he had a keen sense of direction, so he didn't bother to look at his compass.

After walking for a long time, though, he decided he'd better check it. He was surprised to see that the compass indicated he was going west—not east as he had thought. But he was so sure of his own sense of direction that he concluded there must be something wrong with the compass. He was about to throw it away in disgust when this thought came to him: My compass has never lied to me yet; maybe I should believe it. He chose to follow the direction of the compass and soon found his way out of the woods and back home.

There is One who never leads us astray. His instructions are always trustworthy. What God promises, He performs. In 1 Kings 8:56, Solomon told the congregation of Israel that not "one word of all His good promise" had failed. If we think so highly of our own judgment that we refuse to rely on God's Word, we are asking for trouble and will only become more confused. His words have never failed, and they never will. You can count on it!

—*Richard DeHaan*

Fact of Nature

The compass was invented by the Chinese a couple of centuries before Christ. The first historical reference to an explorer who used a compass as a navigational aid is to Chinese ocean voyager Zheng He in the early 1400s.

✳ COMPASS POINT

To presume to know so much that we don't have to trust God is folly.

Einstein's God

Guidebook Reading: Psalm 19:1–6

The heavens declare the glory of God; and the firmament shows His handiwork.
—PSALM 19:1

When the great physicist Albert Einstein was asked if he believed in God, he responded: "We are in the position of a little child entering a huge library filled with books in many languages. The child knows someone must have written those books. It does not know how . . . That, it seems to me, is the attitude of even the most intelligent human beings toward God. We see the universe marvelously arranged and obeying certain laws but only dimly understand these laws." Although Einstein marveled at the design he saw in nature, he did not believe in a personal Creator.

The psalmist shared Einstein's sense of awe about nature but took the next step and believed in the Designer behind the design: "The heavens declare the glory of God; and the firmament shows His handiwork" (Psalm 19:1).

The wonder we feel as we behold our universe should serve as a road sign pointing to the One who created it. The Scriptures tell us, "All things were made through [Christ], and without Him nothing was made that was made" (John 1:3).

Are you struggling in your beliefs? Look up at the stars tonight. In the sky is crafted an amazing road sign pointing to the Designer behind the design.

—*Dennis Fisher*

Fact of Nature

Among the amazing things Einstein did—and most were theoretical findings relating to physics—was to invent a refrigerator that had no moving parts. It was patented in 1926. The patent was purchased by the Electrolux company in 1930.

✴ COMPASS POINT

The intricate design of our world and the awe-inspiring beauty built into this world both point us directly to our creator God.

The Opened Hand

Guidebook Reading: Psalm 145:8–16

You open Your hand and satisfy the desire of every living thing. —Psalm 145:16

Come with me in your imagination to northern Minnesota. From a lovely home overlooking a beautiful lake, I can see stately silver birch trees lining the shore, interspersed with pine, maple, and spruce. A hunter's gun barks in the distance, while a blue jay sings from a shrub in the neighbor's yard. My host says the lake is full of fish, and deer and pheasant abound in the surrounding countryside. This magnificent scene brings to mind the words of David in Psalm 145:16: "You open Your hand and satisfy the desire of every living thing." Yes, a loving Creator provides for the needs of every creature. Charles Spurgeon said that although this verse refers to natural providence, it may also apply to God's grace in the spiritual realm since He is King in both spheres.

Fact *of* Nature

At least 80 kinds of animals call northern Minnesota home, including possums, jackrabbits, cottontail rabbits, woodchucks, eight kinds of squirrels, gophers, beavers, porcupines, black and grizzly bears, raccoons, weasels, otters, foxes, mountain lions, bobcats, elks, deer, and bison.

A train filled with passengers was speeding along its route that crossed a number of rivers. Looking out the window, a child saw the treacherous waters in the distance and was afraid they could not reach the opposite bank. But as they came closer, a bridge appeared and soon the "danger" was behind them. Each time this occurred the youngster was very much disturbed until they had safely crossed to the other side. Finally, however, she leaned back and said with confidence, "Somebody has put bridges for us all the way!"

So too God is constantly providing for the needs of His children. The abundant supply of His goodness and grace is available, and His open hand of blessing is always extended to us. The Creator of the universe is also our Sustainer!

—*Paul Van Gorder*

 COMPASS POINT

Consider how God has provided for you physically, spiritually, monetarily, and in so many other ways.

Good to Be Home

Guidebook Reading: Psalm 73:21–28

You will guide me with Your counsel, and afterward receive me to glory.
—PSALM 73:24

One of my favorite pastimes as a boy was walking the creek behind our home. Those walks were high adventure for me: rocks to skip, birds to watch, dams to build, animal tracks to follow. And if I made it to the mouth of the creek, my dog and I would sit and share lunch while we watched the biplanes land across the lake.

We'd linger as long as we could, but only so long, for my father wanted me home before sunset. The shadows grew long and the hollows got dark fast in the woods. I'd be wishing along the way that I was already home.

Our house sat on a hill behind some trees, but the light was always on until all the family was in. Often my father would be sitting on the back porch, reading the paper, waiting for me. "How did it go?" he would ask. "Pretty good," I'd say. "But it sure is good to be home."

Those memories of walking that creek make me think of another journey—the one I'm making now. It isn't always easy, but I know at the end of it there's a caring Father and my eternal home. I can hardly wait to get there.

I'm expected there. The light is on and my heavenly Father is waiting for me. I suppose He'll ask, just like my father used to, "How did it go?" "Pretty good," I'll say. "But it sure is good to be home."

—*David Roper*

Fact of Nature

In some parts of the US, creek walkers enjoy looking for Native American artifacts, such as arrowheads, either in the water or on the banks where there may have been encampments. One rule of thumb: ethical hunters do not dig; they search the surface only.

✳ COMPASS POINT

At the end of our earthly journey we can look forward to being welcomed home with love and affection.

Scripture Index

Passage	Page
Genesis 1:20	83
Genesis 1:21	93
Genesis 1:31	104
Genesis 2:15	96
Exodus 13:21	97
Exodus 23:12	100
Deuteronomy 11:19	109
2 Samuel 22:2, 3	95
1 Kings 8:56	114
1 Kings 17:4	102
2 Kings 20:15	46
Esther 7:10	64
Job 5:9	89
Job 12:7	40
Job 12:10	107
Job 35:10	24
Job 42:5	67
Psalm 1:2	11
Psalm 19:1	71, 115
Psalm 40:3	60
Psalm 40:5	7
Psalm 73:24	119
Psalm 81:10	45
Psalm 84:12	53
Psalm 87:7	41
Psalm 100:4	43
Psalm 104:24	78
Psalm 104:27	30
Psalm 104:28	8
Psalm 139:14	52
Psalm 145:16	118
Psalm 147:9	17

Passage	Page
Proverbs 3:5	85
Proverbs 7:1, 5	20
Proverbs 16:18	37
Proverbs 20:17	35
Proverbs 29:23	13
Ecclesiastes 3:1	73
Ecclesiastes 3:11	56
Ecclesiastes 7:13	6
Ecclesiastes 11:6	77
Isaiah 1:16	61
Isaiah 24:15	86
Isaiah 40:28–29, 31	5
Isaiah 41:19	103
Isaiah 57:20	16
Isaiah 65:22	38
Jeremiah 8:5	10
Jeremiah 23:29	28
Daniel 6:10	22
Malachi 2:15	90
Matthew 6:26	76
Matthew 7:12	19
Matthew 10:31	106
Matthew 16:16	55
Mark 4:19	84
Luke 15:6	34
John 7:38	108
John 8:44	72
John 16:33	66
Acts 20:24	31

Passage	Page
Romans 1:19	82
Romans 5:3–4	59
Romans 8:13	63
Romans 12:4–6	18
Romans 13:12	58
Romans 15:1	15
1 Corinthians 7:22	47
1 Corinthians 10:12	111
1 Corinthians 15:34	113
Galatians 2:20	94
Galatians 3:3	79
Ephesians 1:4	112
Ephesians 4:27	88
Ephesians 4:31	101
Ephesians 5:8	36

Passage	Page
Philippians 4:14	70
1 Thessalonians 5:19	81
1 Timothy 4:1–2	12
2 Timothy 3:2, 4	48
Titus 3:5	23
Hebrews 11:32–34	49
Hebrews 12:1	33, 65, 91
1 John 3:18	29
Revelation 5:5	68
Revelation 8:10	42
Revelation 21:5	25

Our Daily Bread Writers

Henry Bosch
The first editor of *Our Daily Bread*, Henry had a great appreciation for what nature teaches us about God.

Dave Branon
Through mission trips with teenagers, Dave has seen the extremes of God's creation: the cold majesty of Alaska and the warm beauty of Jamaica. He has written for *Our Daily Bread* since 1988 and has published a number of books.

Bill Crowder
A former pastor who is now an associate Bible teacher for RBC Ministries, Bill enjoys nature on the golf course. He also travels extensively overseas for RBC as a Bible conference teacher.

Dennis DeHaan
When Henry Bosch retired, Dennis became the editor of *Our Daily Bread*. A former pastor, he loved preaching and teaching the Word.

Kurt DeHaan
Kurt was enjoying the outdoors and the joy of exercising when he died in 2003 of a heart attack while taking a lunchtime run. He was editor of *Our Daily Bread* at the time of his death at the age of 50.

Mart DeHaan
President of RBC Ministries for 26 years and now senior advisor of ministry content, Mart learned first about nature from his grandpa, Dr. M. R. DeHaan. Mart enjoys kayaking with his son and fishing with his daughter.

M. R. DeHaan
Founder of RBC Ministries, M. R. DeHaan was a medical doctor who loved to fish, hunt, and tend his substantial garden.

Richard DeHaan
Son of Dr. M. R. DeHaan, Richard was responsible for the ministry's entrance into television. Under his leadership, *Day of Discovery* was first broadcast from one of America's top garden spots, Cypress Gardens, Florida.

Dave Egner
A retired RBC editor, Dave spends as much time as possible in his cabin in Michigan's Upper Peninsula. He's an avid fisherman who loves driving his big old pickup truck.

Dennis Fisher

Transplanted from the West Coast to the Midwest, Dennis enjoys Michigan's beautiful changing seasons. He is research editor at RBC Ministries and managing editor of ChristianCourses.com.

Cindy Hess Kasper

An editor for the RBC publication *Our Daily Journey*, Cindy and her husband, Tom, enjoy the quiet, calm oasis of koi ponds and waterfalls he has constructed in their backyard.

Julie Ackerman Link

Julie observes nature firsthand at her home—watching nesting birds and tending to her backyard garden. She has written a number of books and is a book editor by profession.

David McCasland

Living in Colorado, David cannot escape God's grandeur as displayed in the Rocky Mountains. He and his golden retriever Bonny enjoy getting out and hiking the beauty of Colorado Springs. David has written several books including *Oswald Chambers: Abandoned to God*.

Haddon Robinson

Haddon is former president of Denver Seminary and is the Harold J. Ockenga Distinguished Professor of Preaching at Gordon-Conwell Theological Seminary. He is also the discussion leader for RBC Ministries' *Discover the Word* radio program.

David Roper

Perhaps no RBC writer understands the outdoors like David Roper. His location in Idaho and his interest in hiking and fishing have colored his writing of many books and *Our Daily Bread* articles with strong touches of nature.

Herb Vander Lugt

For many years, Herb was the research editor at RBC Ministries, responsible for checking the biblical accuracy of the RBC materials. A World War II veteran, Herb spent several years as a pastor before his RBC tenure began.

Paul Van Gorder

A writer for *Our Daily Bread* in the 1980s and 1990s, Paul was a noted pastor and Bible teacher, both in the Atlanta area where he lived and through the *Day of Discovery* TV program.

NOTES

NOTES

Note to the Reader

The publisher invites you to share your response to the message of this book by writing Discovery House Publishers, P.O. Box 3566, Grand Rapids, MI 49501, U.S.A. For information about other Discovery House books, music, videos, or DVDs, contact us at the same address or call 1-800-653-8333. Find us on the Internet at www.dhp.org or send an e-mail to books@dhp.org.